Christian Moerlein

Christian Moerlein

Christian Moerlein

The Man
and
His Brewery

by

Don Heinrich Tolzmann

Foreword by

Gregory Hardman

Little Miami Publishing Co.
Milford, Ohio
2012

Little Miami Publishing Co.
P.O. Box 588
Milford, Ohio 45150-0588
www.littlemiamibooks.com

Printed in the United States of America on acid-free paper.

ISBN-13: 978-1-932250-99-2
ISBN-10: 1-932250-99-9

Library of Congress Control Number: 2012937352

Contents

Foreword

WHEN IT WAS ANNOUNCED the brand rights of the Christian Moerlein Brewing Company had been purchased by me, greater Cincinnati resident Gregory Hardman on March 1, 2004, a media flurry ensued. After being owned by out-of-towners for a short period of time, Christian Moerlein, a brand that represented so much to Cincinnati's grand brewing heritage and craft beer future was coming back home. This announcement followed my almost eighteen-year career with Warsteiner Brauerei of Warstein, Germany, at their wholly owned subsidiary, Warsteiner Importers Agency.

During my tenure at Warsteiner, I developed great friendships from many colleagues around the world, especially from Germany. One in particular, Hermann Boerger, former export director at Warsteiner who I had the pleasure of working with for eight years during the time that I was president and CEO of their North American Operations, had left Warsteiner Brauerei to pursue other interests in the beverage industry. Having transitioned to the Geschäftsführung Vertrieb (chief of sales) for the Maisel Brauerei, Hermann and I kept in contact with each other.

On one such occasion, when I told Hermann that I had left Warsteiner, we bonded over our new career paths. Sharing what we had in store for the future, I mentioned that I had bought a brand by the name of Christian Moerlein, and that I planned to reopen a brewery that dated back to 1853. Immediately, Hermann responded, "We have a Mr. Moerlein that works at the brewery!" Inquisitively, I thought *that's interesting; Moerlein isn't the equivalent of a common name in America, such as "Smith" or "Jones."* I continued on with my story, explaining what my four-phase plan would be to return the Christian Moerlein brand and brewing company to its rightful position in Cincinnati brewing lore.

Having been neglected and purchased by out-of-town owners in 1999, phase number one was to return the local ownership of the Christian Moerlein brand to Cincinnati. Second, to make the brand more relevant to today's consumers, as this was the first American beer to pass the German Purity Law, known as the Reinheitsgebot, also known as a pioneer craft brand of today's craft beer movement. Third, to open local brewing operations in Cincinnati's Over-the-Rhine Brewing District, which was the original location where Christian Moerlein was once brewed. And lastly, to open the Christian Moerlein Lager House on the banks of the Ohio River; where beer once traveled during the mid-nineteenth century, from the Brewery District, down Main Street, to the port of Cincinnati. Hermann gave his feedback, saying that those were lofty goals, but he had all the confidence in the world that I would be able to accomplish them.

He then explained his career path with the Maisel Brauerei and that it was located in the Bavarian city of Bayreuth, in the Franconia region of Germany, and was the home of Wagner, a well-known German composer and conductor. Being the "technology sleuth" that I am, I immediately searched a map of Germany on my computer to find the location of Bayreuth. While doing this, I was intrigued by this location, as it sounded very familiar to the history and place where Christian Moerlein once lived.

At that moment, I said to Hermann, "Christian Moerlein was born in a small village called Truppach." Hermann says to me, "Gregory, Truppach is around eight kilometers from the brewery." I said,

"Wow, what a coincidence! I wonder if the Mr. Moerlein at the Maisel Brauerei is related to Christian Moerlein, the famous Cincinnati beer baron." Hermann said that he would check with Mr. Moerlein, as well as mention this to Oscar Maisel, the reigning patriarch of the Maisel Brauerei.

Some weeks later, I communicated with Hermann again. He mentioned to me that he had spoken with Oscar Maisel about this coincidence, and he forwarded to me a copy of Christian Moerlein's birth certificate obtained by Mr. Maisel from Truppach. He assured me that this was the same man that was Cincinnati's great brewer, who was born May 13, 1818. In 2008, I was invited to speak at a beverage conference in London, England. Taking advantage of this opportunity, I decided to book a trip to see my former colleague and friend Hermann at the Maisel Brauerei in Bayreuth.

Upon arriving, I was introduced to Mr. Moerlein, who in my opinion had a striking resemblance to the photographs that I had seen of Christian Moerlein; however, he had no knowledge of the accomplishments of Christian Moerlein, or any connection to his possible ancestral link. Later that afternoon, I asked Hermann if I could borrow his BMW to take a drive out to Truppach, which was very close to the Brauerei. Hermann, known for having a heavy foot, was keenly aware of my pension for wanting to travel the autobahn at high rates of speed. He reminded me that there is no autobahn between Truppach and Bayreuth; though the two-lane road to Truppach didn't hinder my ability to achieve speed.

Upon my rapid arrival, a noticeable farmhouse, obviously built in the eighteenth century, caught my eye from the left side of the road. My mind raced; looking at that house, I literally thought *Christian Moerlein probably lived in that house growing up.* Later I learned Christian Moerlein, in fact, did live in that exact house. I then pulled off onto the side roads of the village, trying to engage locals in order to investigate if any Moerleins still lived in the area. Unfortunately, the folks that I encountered had no knowledge of the Moerlein family, but they directed me to the local Gasthaus bar to possibly obtain more information. While driving by the Gasthaus, I discovered that it was closed, and began to turn around.

The Truppach city limits sign on the other side of the road glared at me. I decided to stop and take a picture, and at that moment the thought occurred to me that for such a tiny village, it was amazing that a young, German immigrant named Christian Moerlein would have traveled so far to come to Cincinnati, seeking his fortune. His story, being the quintessential German-American immigrant experience, had never been told in robust detail. That's when it occurred to me that I needed to call my long-time friend, Don Heinrich Tolzmann, an author of many German-American cultural books, to inform him that this is a story worthy of telling. I proceeded to give Don a call from Germany, compelling him to write the story of Christian Moerlein. Don said, "Let's meet for a Moerlein when you get back from Germany to discuss."

Shortly after I returned to Cincinnati, Don and I met for that Christian Moerlein beer and discussed what I had experienced, and to explain to him why I was fascinated with Christian Moerlein's story. For me, it was amazing how much Christian Moerlein achieved in Cincinnati and around the world during his lifetime and at the same time being from a small town in Germany. Where did he get this motivation to leave Truppach to become Cincinnati's greatest beer baron? Don quickly became interested as well, and he wrote this book seeing my keen interest for learning more about Christian Moerlein the man and his life. I couldn't think of a more appropriate person to bring this story to life, since it is such an important story to be told for Cincinnati's grand brewing traditions.

Gregory Hardman
President and CEO
Christian Moerlein Brewing Company

Introduction

Amerika, du hast es besser,
Als unser Kontinent, der alte,
Hast keine verfallenen Schlösser
Und keine Basalte.

Dich stört nicht im Innern
Zu lebendiger Zeit
Unnützes Erinnern
Und vergeblicher Streit

————

America, you are better off
Than is our old continent.
You have no ruined castles
And no basalt cliffs.

In vital times
You are not disturbed in your heart
By useless memories
And by fruitless quarrels.

— Johann Wolfgang von Goethe[1]

"America, you are better off" is the way Goethe described America in the early nineteenth century and his description no doubt resonated with many Germans after the long, hard years of the Napoleonic wars. Not surprisingly, the United States acquired a reputation in the German states as "*das Land der unbegrenzten Möglichkeiten*," (the land of unlimited possibilities), causing millions to seek their luck in the New World. One of them was Christian Moerlein (1818–97) whose life represents a classic example of the immigrant success story, demonstrating that one really could "make it" in America by means of hard work, thrift, and persistence. In telling his story my goal has been to follow the path he took in realizing his vision and version of the American Dream by founding the Christian Moerlein Brewing Company.

Christian Moerlein, the Man and His Brewery explains the phenomenal success his company attained and the legendary status he enjoys in the annals of Cincinnati's German brewing heritage as its foremost beer baron. Moerlein's biography also reveals the importance of his family for the growth and development of his company. His son George, who played a major role in the development of the brewery, will, therefore, receive detailed attention, as will to a lesser extent, other members of his family.

Also included are several appendices to help understand the life and times of Christian Moerlein and his brewery. Appendix A deals with "Fellow Beer Barons" and provides translations from local German-American histories of the biographies of several Cincinnati German beer barons for comparison with Moerlein's life story. Appendix B has information on "Lager Beer History" for those who would like to know more about the brew known as "liquid bread" that came to America by means of the German immigrations of the nineteenth century. Appendix C focuses on "Major Breweries in Greater Cincinnati," identifying the leading companies before Prohibition. Finally, Appendix D deals with "Related Industries," covering barrel making, and brass and copper manufacturing.

CHAPTER 1

A Self-Made Man

ALMOST EVERYONE IN THE GREATER CINCINNATI area has heard the name of Christian Moerlein. His name is a legendary part of Cincinnati's German brewing history and heritage, but who was he and what was he like? And how did he become one of the major brewers of the region and the nation? We know his name, but not the man. Is there more to it than that he was the legendary beer baron of Cincinnati's Over-the-Rhine district who produced some of the best brews in the country?

Because Christian Moerlein left no journals, letters, or papers, answering these questions is no easy matter. Fortunately, several histories of Cincinnati are available in German and English that provide us with biographical information about him. From them we can recount the basic dates, facts, and events of his life and bring the images of him into focus that they project.

An Early Biography

In 1878, when Christian Moerlein was sixty years old, Armin Tenner published a history of the Cincinnati Germans, *Cincinnati Sonst und*

Jetzt (*Cincinnati Then and Now*), which provides a history of German immigration and settlement in Cincinnati.[1] A substantial volume consisting of almost five hundred pages, it is particularly valuable because of the biographical directory it contains. This consists of biographies ranging in length from one to several pages, often including illustrations of the individuals covered. All had in some way made their mark on the history of the region and attained a degree of success in their particular field of endeavor, which served as the basic criteria for inclusion in this work.

Tenner's history continues to serve as an index of the leading figures in the history of Cincinnati's German element with a wealth of biographical information, but has never been translated. Rather than merely listing brief biographical data as to birth and death dates, among other things, Tenner provides interestingly written and informative biographical essays on prominent Cincinnati Germans, many of whom he most likely knew or had spoken with for the completion of this work.

Works focusing on successful individuals are commonly as well as irreverently known as "mug books," because they provide illustrations, or "mug shots" along with the biographies. What is particularly useful about them is not just the biographical information they provide, but also the character traits they illuminate for the purpose of explaining how the prominent persons covered had attained success. Therefore, they serve a two-fold purpose. First, they aim to provide biographical information, but, second, they also tend to send a message about what can be learned from those who have attained success in life. Such works, of course, aimed to sing a song of praise, but the biographies did have to ring true and stick to the facts if they were to find community-wide acceptance.

By highlighting the life stories of successful German-Americans such works also aimed to tell the story of German contributions to the making of America and underscore the pride felt in German-American achievements. The biographies were crafted to serve as models for those interested in climbing the ladder of success by following in the tracks of their compatriots, past and present. A work like Tenner's, therefore, reads like a guidebook to success.

By the 1870s, Christian Moerlein had definitely accomplished a great deal. In 1878, he had been in America for thirty-seven years. His life had been a phenomenal success story of how an immigrant had arrived in America at the age of twenty-three with only a few dollars his pockets, and had risen to become one of the most successful businessmen, not only in Cincinnati but the entire country as well. In the process, he built a family business that functioned like a dynasty with a brewing empire in the Over-the-Rhine district of Cincinnati.

Armin Tenner's biography of Christian Moerlein, as translated from the German, provides us with the basic biographical information about his life and work, and in so doing helps bring a personal image of him into focus.[2]

Christian Moerlein
by Armin Tenner

The man whose name stands at the head of this article represents another example of German industriousness. Like hundreds of Cincinnatians who made it here by means of hard work, he came here without any knowledge of the English language and ignorant as well of American social and business customs and traditions. Since that time, he has become a man of great wealth and the owner of a business that provides hundreds with employment. In attaining this goal, he surpassed thousands of Americans who did not have to deal with the difficulties we have already alluded to.

It is not the case that he possessed more talents than others, but rather that he was satisfied with beginning at the lowest rung of the ladder, slowly and steadily working his way to the top, and also because it never entered his mind to try to attain wealth without practicing the virtue of thriftiness. In this regard, he has provided a sterling example for all.[3]

Christian Moerlein, the son of Conrad Moerlein, was born on 13 May 1818 at Truppach in Bavaria. After attending the village school to the age of thirteen, he made the first important decision in his active life in that he commenced working as a blacksmith apprentice and as a worker on the farm of his father. During the winter months, he learned the trade of brewing from his uncle, thereby laying the foundation for his later business enterprise here, and one on which Cincinnati can look back on with great pleasure.

The times passed by with these various occupations till he had reached the age of eighteen, and then came the time for five further years of *Lehrjahre* (years of apprenticeship) that are required of German tradesmen. During this time, he earned one Prussian thaler, or dollar per week. The thought of becoming independent awoke in him as he completed his apprenticeship years, as did the idea of establishing a household of his own.[4] However, the salary of one thaler weekly made this impossible and, moreover, did not even provide enough for him to acquire his own clothing.

In view of this situation, his father offered him one hundred gulden—about forty dollars—which the youth gladly accepted, and then in good spirits "with a flower in his hat and staff in hand" made his way on foot to Bremen, located some three hundred miles away.[5] Here and there he found employment, thereby providing himself with bed and boarding along the way. Tired and worn out, he arrived in Bremen on St. John the Baptist Day, 24 June 1841. Three weeks later the ship disembarked that brought him to America. After a terrible trip lasting fifty-eight days, he arrived in Baltimore, sick from the deprivations of the journey.[6]

On his arrival in America his funds consisted of twelve dollars, of which he then had to expend eight dollars for a ticket by canal and train to Pittsburgh, Pennsylvania. On not finding work, he then moved on to Wheeling, [West] Virginia. By now, he had all of fifty cents in his pocket, and all attempts at finding a job remained without success. As Moerlein was about to turn his back on Wheeling and move on across the bridge to the Ohio side of the Ohio River, a German countryman got him a job with a slaveholder for seventy-five cents daily. Moerlein stayed there for a week, working with a threshing machine.

However, he then decided to get on the road again with a back-pack on his back, and headed out for Portsmouth, Ohio, where he had some acquaintances.[7] On the way, he again sought work, finding a job as a blacksmith, but since his boss understood no German, and he no English, there was no chance here for anything permanent, so we again find him on the road again.

At first, he found work in Hendricksburg, Ohio, and to be sure, for the enormous salary of seven dollars monthly, a wage which gradually rose to fifteen dollars. In 1842, he returned to Wheeling, and from there moved on to Cincinnati, arriving there on the 1st of April. Here he found his first job digging a cellar at Jackson Hill. He earned 50 cents daily, of which he spent half daily for his meals, so that when a rainy day came, he would have funds available to cover his expenses.

Moerlein in the meantime got a job in his own trade as a black-smith not far from the Brighton House, where he remained till October of that year. He then began his own business on Findlay Street. In the following year, 1843, he married Sophie Adams, a native of Strass-burg in Alsace-Lorraine. Favored with good fortune in business, he was soon able to have a home built on Elm Street alongside his black-smith business. In a short time, his business flourished to the extent that he was able to employ from six to ten workers.

During the cholera epidemic of 1849, he lost his beloved wife, which left him with the three surviving children.[8] One died the same year, the second in 1853. Moerlein remarried in 1849 to Barbara Oeh, also a native of Germany, who bore the family a total of nine children. Of them a total of six are still alive. John, from the first marriage, as well as George and Jacob are currently all in their father's business.

In 1853 Moerlein sold his blacksmith business and entered a partnership with Adam Dillmann to establish a brewery at the site of where his blacksmith company had been located. Their first beer was sold on 1 March 1854, but in the following year Dillmann passed away, leaving the business in the hands of Moerlein as its sole owner. Moerlein then partnered with the brewer Conrad Windisch, and business expanded annually.[9] In the winter of 1855/56, they brewed their first lager beer—two thousand barrels. In four years, production had grown to a total of ten thousand barrels annually, but still, of course, had not reached what it has now attained.

In 1866, they brewed a total of 26,500 barrels of beer, an astonishing amount of beer for the time. In September of that year, Moerlein bought out his partner for $130,000. Two years later, he built the main building for his brewery, located on the east side of Elm Street, where he also had cellars constructed with a capacity of holding 9,000 barrels of beer. Additionally, four new cellars were added later, so that a total of 15,000 barrels of beer could be stored altogether.

The main building was four stories high, and its dimensions were 120 feet wide in the front of the building, and 110 feet in depth. During the summer of 1872, Moerlein built more cellars, each holding a total of 1,000 barrels of beer, and then built an icehouse on top of them in 1876 in the style of the main brewery building. This was 80 feet wide by 100 feet in depth. In the first floor it had a gigantic lager beer cellar, in the second an equally spacious room for fermentation, and in the third a large icehouse reaching all the way to the roof. Altogether, there was room at the brewery for a total of 45,000 barrels of beer.

At the building site of the old brewery on the west side of Elm Street a substantial malt house was built in 1873 that was 100 feet wide and 100 feet in depth. The storage area held a total of 173,000 bushels of barley. Cooperage work was done mainly on site at the brewery. Altogether, there were 110 workers (a total of 250 people with families included) that were supported by the brewery. However, many more were also employed on a daily basis. The brewery also had stalls for the stabling of forty-five horses.

In 1864, Moerlein had three homes built at Fifteenth and Elm Streets, and under them had cellars constructed that held 3,000 barrels of beer. Annual sales by 1866 had now reached 25,000 barrels of beer, and currently are at the amount of 100,000 barrels.

The actual key to Moerlein's success is undoubtedly his character, his untiring energy, his firm resolve in all his plans, his ability to oversee employees, his wealth, his good insight in his business and trade, and his ability to swiftly respond to favorable circumstances. He is one of those of whom we say that in everything they do, they have good fortune. Moerlein is not unwilling to help those who are in need, but prefers to help others help themselves, rather than merely make a donation.

Altogether, he is a man who knows how to appreciate the beauties of life. He is a sociable person, when not occupied with the concerns of his business. His outstanding abilities administering and managing such a large company have also resulted in his often being appointed to a number of important public offices.

An Image Emerges

In this first lengthy biography of Moerlein, Tenner brings together not only the essential facts about Christian Moerlein, but also a description of the character traits by which he was known. He writes that Moerlein "represents another example of German industriousness." And, he came here "without any knowledge of the English language and ignorant as well of American social and business customs and traditions." Nevertheless, he became "a man of great wealth and the owner of a business that provides hundreds with employment." Especially noteworthy is the fact that "In attaining this goal, he surpassed thousands of Americans who did not have to deal with the difficulties we have already alluded to." He was no more talented than others, according to Tenner, but began at the bottom of the ladder "slowly and steadily working his way to the top," always practicing "the virtue of thriftiness." As a result, he provides "a sterling example for all."

Tenner concludes his biography by noting that the key to Moerlein's success was "undoubtedly his character, his untiring energy, his firm resolve in all his plans, his ability to oversee employees, his wealth, his good insight in his business and trade, and his ability to swiftly respond to favorable circumstances." He was the kind of person "for whom we say that in everything they do, they have good fortune." He also emphasizes Moerlein's philanthropic nature, explaining that "Moerlein is not unwilling to help those who are in need, but prefers to help others help themselves, rather than merely make a donation."

Tenner further amplifies his account by commenting that "Altogether, he [Moerlein] is a man who knows how to appreciate the beauties of life. He is a sociable person, when not occupied with the concerns of his business." And, with regard to the latter, he notes that "His outstanding abilities administering and managing such a large company have also resulted in his often being appointed to a number of important public offices."

CHAPTER 2

A Sterling Example

A Recurrent Theme

TEN YEARS AFTER TENNER'S HISTORY, another history of the Cincinnati Germans appeared: Max Burgheim's *Cincinnati in Wort und Bild* (1888) (*Cincinnati in Word and Picture*). This provides further insight into the kind of person Moerlein was and builds on the biography of Tenner. Although it contains the same basic biographical data, Burgheim provides some additional information that brings us closer to an understanding of Moerlein. He mentions, for example, that Moerlein had taken an interest in America as the land of opportunity and that this was a factor motivating him to immigrate to the United States.

Burgheim also emphasizes the success story theme that was touched on by Tenner. He refers to Moerlein as one of the best-known German-Americans in the country, whose name is known north and south, east and west. He notes that German-Americans took special pride in him as a self-made man, who had become a success in his new homeland.

Christian Moerlein is one of the most important businessmen

in Cincinnati, well known, highly regarded and respected by everyone. Locals as well as others are amazed at the success of this man, who rose from the most modest beginnings to become the king of his industry, acquiring a princely fortune in the process.[1]

Burgheim also comments that the real and lasting monument established by Moerlein was not his brewing company, but rather "the sterling example" he provided of what one could attain in America by means of hard work, thrift, and persistence. Here Burgheim uses the very same terminology as did Tenner to describe him, thus endorsing and reiterating this description of him. According to Burgheim, Moerlein's success flowed from his impeccable character, his untiring energy, his decisiveness and outstanding administrative skills, all of which set him apart from others and won him widespread recognition and honor. Such comments underscore the recurrent theme of Moerlein as an immigrant success story and the lessons his life might have for others.

The success story theme was, of course, not confined to German-American histories, but can also be found in the English-language histories of the time. One such work is the *History of Cincinnati and Hamilton County, Ohio*, published in 1894. It contains a directory of breweries, which provides us with another biography of Moerlein. It also conveys the success story theme found in local histories, demonstrating that the Moerlein success story was one that was widely recognized throughout the region. The history describes him as "an example of what young men may accomplish in this country when they bring to their task industry, frugality and high integrity of purpose." It then provides a biography of Moerlein interwoven with the history of his company.

From *History of Cincinnati and Hamilton County, Ohio*

The Cincinnati brewery covering the largest area of ground is owned and operated by the Christian Moerlein Brewing Company. The office of the company is situated on Elm Street, while right opposite is the immense plant where the beer is manufactured.

The success of the firm is due to the indefatigable efforts of Christian Moerlein, who was born in Germany in 1818. Believing that he could better his condition in this country he crossed the ocean, landing in Ohio in 1841, with very little money. A year later he became a resident of the Queen City. He established a blacksmith shop on the west side of Elm Street, near McMicken Avenue, and upon the ground, where many a hard stroke was made, is the malt-house of the well-known brewery. Fortune smiled upon him. In a few years he had established a large and lucrative business, and in 1853 he concluded to go into the business at which he has accumulated such a deserving fortune.

Very few people then thought that Mr. Moerlein, who was brewing about three barrels a day, would at this time be at the head of one of the biggest breweries in the country. It required hard work to accomplish the object in view. He was a business man in every sense of the word. Being a man of good judgment, and farseeing, he took advantage of every opportunity that afforded itself, and it was not long before he had acquired the reputation of being one of the shrewdest men in his line of business. He is often sought after for advice, and is always ready and willing to lend a helping hand. He is charitably inclined, but never cares to tell of his many kindly acts.

Mr. Moerlein's first partner was Mr. Dillmann. At his death, in 1854, Mr. Windisch became associated with him, and remained a member of the firm until 1866, when his interests were purchased by Mr. Moerlein.

In 1881 the Christian Moerlein Brewing Company was formed with a capital stock of $1,000,000 paid in. In 1853 common beer was brewed, in 1856 lager beer was introduced and, in 1864 common beer was discontinued. The output in 1853 was 1,000 barrels; in 1860, 20,000 barrels; in 1870, 60,000 barrels; in 1880, 100,000 barrels, and the steady increase since has placed this brewery as the largest one in the State of Ohio, and one of the largest in the United States. During all these years of competition, and during the panics of 1857 and 1873, the reputation of this house, as far as the finances are concerned, was never questioned. It is now on as solid a basis as it ever has been.

When first reorganized under the articles of incorporation, in 1881, the officers were as follows: Christian Moerlein, president; George Moerlein, vice-president, John Goetz, Jr., secretary; Jacob Moerlein, treasurer; John Moerlein, general superintendent. After the death of George Moerlein, August 31, 1891, the following officers were elected September 15, 1891: Christian Moerlein, president; John Moerlein, first vice-president and general manager; John Goetz, Jr., second vice-president; Jacob Moerlein, treasurer; William Moerlein, secretary.

They are all well known as efficient officers and business men. The capacity of their immense establishment is 500,000 barrels a year. The machinery is of the modern pattern. In the last twelve years a great many changes have been made in the way of erecting buildings and cellars, and the second largest refrigerating machine plan in the United States can be seen here.[2]

The 1894 history then concludes by noting that Moerlein had commented recently with great pride that Cincinnati, with its twenty-three breweries, ranked seventh in the United States as a beer brewing center. He no doubt also took great pride in the fact that his company had contributed greatly to putting Cincinnati on the beer-brewing map nationally.

A Success Story

Recognition of Moerlein's achievements was not confined to biographical works of the region. In 1896, a year before his death, he was included in a biographical work titled *America's Successful Men of Affairs: An Encyclopedia of Contemporaneous Biography*, edited by Henry Hall and published by the *New York Tribune*. This massive two-volume work provides an impressive array of approximately two thousand biographies "of the master spirits of the business world in the United States at large." It states that "the key note of this work is success in business and practical affairs." It also emphasized that

> The examples of success in this work should prove a strong incentive to the capable youth of America to make the most of their lives, to begin in youth to cultivate habits of thrift and thoroughness, and to lay, even before attaining their majority, the sound basis of character, practical sense, energy, and integrity, without which a lasting success in affairs is practically impossible.[3]

The biographical entry for Moerlein provides much of the same biographical information that has been covered thus far, but it does emphasize that the key to his success story was "hard work and self-denial." It also provides a few other details regarding some of his affiliations, noting that "Mr. Moerlein is trustee of the Cincinnati Water Works and connected with the German National Bank and nearly all the charitable institutions in the city."[4] The most important item to take note of with regard to this biographical entry is that Moerlein was included in such an encyclopedia of successful businessmen, thereby demonstrating his national reputation.

An Image Defined

Building on the work of Tenner, Burgheim sharpens the focus of Moerlein's image, referring to him similarly as a "sterling example" of a self-made man. He calls him one of the best known German-Americans of the time, emphasizing that by means of hard work, thrift, and persistence he had become "the king of his industry." Moerlein was now also being covered in the English-language histories of the area as well.

And the 1894 English-language history, *History of Cincinnati and Hamilton County*, described Moerlein as "an example of what young men may accomplish in this country when they bring to their task industry, frugality and high integrity of purpose." It states that the success of the Moerlein Brewing Company was "due to the indefatigable efforts" of Moerlein and that "hard work" was required to attain success. Additionally, it notes that "Being a man of good judgment, and farseeing, he took advantage of every opportunity that afforded itself, and it was not long before he had acquired the reputation of being one of the shrewdest men in his line of business." This history also mentions his philanthropic endeavors by noting that Moerlein was "always ready and willing to lend a helping hand. He is charitably inclined, but never cares to tell of his many acts." Finally, Moerlein's inclusion in a national biographical encyclopedia of successful businessmen underscores the recognition that he had attained by the latter decades of the nineteenth century.

By the close of the nineteenth century, Moerlein's image had vividly come into focus as that of a "sterling example" of a self-made man. Although justifiably called the "the king of his industry," he also was without question Cincinnati's foremost beer baron of the Over-the-Rhine district. All in all, a phenomenal immigrant success story.

Moerlein Brewery on Elm Street.

CHAPTER 3

A Premier Beer Baron

Family and Company

BY THE LATTER DECADES OF THE NINETEENTH CENTURY, Christian Moerlein had "made it" in America and occupied an honored and respected place in the community, as is clearly and glowingly reflected in descriptions of him in German- and English-language histories and directories. Within a matter of a few decades, he had founded a business that had become one of the major breweries in the region and the nation. A key element to its success was that it was based on family. This was the typical modus operandi not only for other breweries, but also for other German-American businesses as well. They drew their strength from close-knit families, with an active role in the company hierarchy for each member of the family.

Brewers were known for the pride they took in their product as well as their families. They were intensely loyal to family and business. They reigned over their brewing empires much like dynasties, such as the Busch family in Saint Louis, often intermarrying with other brewing families as well. And their sons often studied their trade at brewing academies in the United States or Germany. It is, therefore, not surprising that the organizational chart of the Moerlein Brewing Company mirrored that of the Moerlein family tree. Both were identical.

Together with his first wife, Sophia (Adams) Moerlein (1825–49), whom he married in 1843, Christian Moerlein had three children:

Jacob (1844–53)

John Christian (1846–1921)

Christina (1848–49)

Of these children, two died of the cholera epidemic as did Moerlein's first wife, with only the son John surviving, and later becoming president of the brewery.

Together with his second wife, Barbara (Oeh) Moerlein (1827–1903), whom he married in 1849, Christian Moerlein had nine children:

Magdalena (1850–1930)—known as Lena

John George (1852–91)—known as George

Jacob (1855–1912)

Anna Catherine (1857–1861)

Elizabeth (1860–1925)—known as Lizzy

Christian, Jr., 1863–65

Wilhelm (1866–96)

Emma (1868–1928)

Emilie (1872–74)

Of his children, seven were directly or indirectly involved with the brewery. Four of his sons became part of the management team: John, George, Wilhelm, and Jacob. His daughter Magdalena married a Columbus, Ohio, brewer, Conrad Born. And his daughter Elizabeth married John Goetz, Jr., who was part of the management team of the Moerlein Brewing Company. Daughter Emma remained single and lived at the Moerlein family home, thus strengthening the home base. Together, they formed the dynasty that held the Moerlein brewing empire aloft down to the time of Prohibition. A generous father, Moerlein gave his children fifty thousand dollars in company stock in 1881 and twenty-five thousand dollars more in 1886 on his sixty-eighth birthday.

Community Life

An integral part of German-American family life was membership in an Over-the-Rhine congregation. As pillars of the business community, Over-the-Rhine brewing families strongly supported the churches they belonged to, serving on boards of trustees and donating generously to them. Thus they played an important role not only in the business life of the area, but also in the community's religious life as well.

Although Bavaria is predominantly Catholic, Moerlein came from the northern part of Bavaria known as Franconia, which is predominantly Evangelical-Lutheran. In Cincinnati, Moerlein and his first wife joined a German Evangelical church located at Elm and Liberty Streets, the Saint Mattheus Church, which was founded in 1841. Their membership probably dates from the year of their marriage (1843), as church records indicate that their three children were all baptized there. Jacob was baptized there (24 November 1844), followed by the baptisms of John (6 September 1846), and Christina (10 November 1848). Christina's godparents Friedrich and Christine Muhlhauser came from the Muhlhauser brewing family, an indication of the close-knit nature of relations among the brewing families of the area.

In 1890, the Moerleins were among the founding members of a newly formed congregation, which constructed the Philippus Church, a beautiful red-brick Gothic-style structure, located on West McMicken Avenue. Their membership in this church makes a statement about the importance of their faith. The Moerleins were part of a group that withdrew from Saint Mattheus as a result of disagreements regarding the use of literature from the Eden Publishing House in Saint Louis, which was the publishing house of the German Evangelical Synod of North America. Congregations of this synod varied theologically, ranging from a conservative orthodoxy to a liberal kind of rationalism. Many members of Saint Mattheus, including the pastor, felt that the literature published by the Eden Publishing House tended too much toward the latter position, thus leading to a schism of the church.

Matters came to a head in 1890 when Saint Mattheus locked its doors not only on its Sunday school staff and students, but also its pastor. Rev. Dr. Jacob Pistor had served as pastor of the congregation since 1881, but the lockout caused him and others to form a new congregation, the Philippus Church, which today belongs to the United Church of Christ. That the Moerleins belonged to the group that helped found the new church might best be viewed as a move reflecting Moerlein's Lutheran origins in Franconia and his feeling that the newly formed German Evangelical congregation was more in line with them. Church life for the Moerlein family, therefore, meant more than nominal membership in a congregation.

Churches played an important role not only in terms of the religious life of their members, but also in their social, cultural, and educational life as well, sponsoring a wide variety of programs and activities throughout the year. They also played a major role in the preservation of the German language. They held services in German and provided Sunday school and confirmation classes in German for the youth of their congregations. Ministers had studied at seminaries either in the United States or Germany, serving not only as spiritual role models for members of their congregations, but also taking an active role in the life of the community and often were the best educated members of their congregations.

Today, the Philippus Church is one of the noteworthy landmarks in Over-the-Rhine, especially because of its "Finger to Heaven." This is a clenched golden hand with the index finger pointing to heaven that is atop the steeple of the church. This was placed there at the direction of Reverend Doctor Pistor, thus making a symbolic statement of faith.

Aside from church life, Moerlein also belonged to seven German-American societies: the North Cincinnati Turnverein, the Bavarian Beneficial Society, the German Pioneer Society, the Humboldt Chapter, the Hanselmann Lodge, Jefferson Lodge, and the German Home for the Elderly. Moerlein was one of the founding members of the latter, which maintained a home for the elderly and was mainly supported by members of the German-American business elite in

The Moerlein family belonged to the Philippus Church.

Cincinnati. Membership in the Bavarian Beneficial Society made sense, as Moerlein was from Bavaria. And, the North Cincinnati Turnverein was located not that far from Moerlein's uptown home. It was a society that influential members of the German-American community belonged to, as well as non-Germans, such as William Howard Taft, who felt it politically advisable to join its ranks.

135th anniversary history of the Bavarian Beneficial Society.
Moerlein was a member of this society.

Extracurricular Activities

In addition to the brewing business, Moerlein was also involved in several other business ventures unrelated to the brewing industry. In 1884, he invested in the Cincinnati Cremation Company located at what is now 525 Martin Luther King, Jr., Drive in Clifton. The idea behind this company apparently came from the belief that cremation would prevent the spread of disease and most likely had its origins in the cholera epidemic of the nineteenth century, which had taken the life of Moerlein's first wife. It probably also was related to another business venture—the Southern Granite Company. This was owned by his son George Moerlein (president of the company); son-in-law John Goetz, Jr.; and J. Adolf Eberhard. The former company provided cremations and the latter gravestones, making for an interesting and interrelated business combination.

Christian Moerlein himself was also said to have held investments in silver mines out West, where there apparently was a mine shaft known as the "Moerlein shaft." These sideline business investments demonstrated that although the primary business was brewing the family also held some other areas of interest and was able to diversify its holdings as a result of the profit-making nature of the brewery. The family had built a highly successful brewing empire and could now branch out into other areas. However, like the brewery, these endeavors were largely family affairs, involving several members of the family working together as a team.

Later Years

What about the later years of Christian Moerlein? For the answer, we can turn to another history of the Cincinnati Germans, *Cincinnati und sein Deutschthum* (1901) (*Cincinnati and its Germandom*). Although briefer than the previous works already cited, it does follow the same line of thought in viewing Moerlein as the embodiment of the self-made man who was fully engaged and involved with his company right up to the last days of his life.

Until the very end, he remained active in his company; every day, if his age permitted, he made the short distance from his home to his brewery to take care of business matters, etc. The last time he was seen in his office was only a few days before his death. As an almost 80 year old man, he finally closed his eyes to rest from a life that was full of toil and work, but so rich in success.[1]

The cause of death for Christian Moerlein (14 May 1897), which was one day after his seventy-ninth birthday, was described as "congestion of the brain."[2] His funeral service took place at the Moerlein home on Ohio Avenue, 18 May 1897, with services conducted by Rev. Emil K. L. Schmidt of Saint Mattheus and Reverend Doctor Pistor of Philippus. Burial took place thereafter at Spring Grove Cemetery. The pallbearers for Moerlein included his sons John and Jacob and son-in-law John Goetz, Jr. Several German societies sent delegations, including the North Cincinnati Turnverein, the Hanselmann Lodge, the German Pioneer Society, the Bavarian Beneficial Society, the Humboldt Chapter, and the Jefferson Lodge. And the University of Cincinnati issued a resolution in honor of Moerlein as well.

In an obituary published in its annual report for 1897, the German Pioneer Society of Cincinnati expressed the hope that Cincinnati would never lack individuals, such as Christian Moerlein, who had been "one of the main supporters of the German element" and whose life was almost identical with and had contributed so much to the growth and development of the city of Cincinnati." It described his life not only as "noteworthy," but also as a "rarity" due to his many achievements in business and the fact that he had lived a long and healthy life with a sound mind right up to the time of his death. Moreover, it noted that Moerlein was well known for his "simplicity, decency, cordiality, and kindness," and that these character traits had been enhanced, not diminished by his success in business affairs. It also emphasized that his life demonstrated that the best way to get ahead in life was by means of hard work and persistence, and that these traits had characterized the life of Moerlein, who was well known for his determination, will power, energy, and his "indestructible sense of honesty and self-esteem."[3]

In an obituary in its annual report for 1897, the Cincinnati Chamber of Commerce and Merchant's Exchange reported,

> For nearly thirty years, he was a member of the Chamber of Commerce, and by his death, it has lost one of its oldest, staunchest and most honored friends, and the city of Cincinnati a public spirited, philanthropic and widely esteemed citizen.
>
> By his energy, indomitable will and integrity, he built up a large and prosperous business, and by his uniformly considerate, affable and just treatment toward all who came in contact with him, he endeared himself to every one, and enjoyed a deserved and widespread popularity.
>
> Mr. Moerlein was a modest man of exemplary character, avoiding display or publicity; he contributed liberally to charities, public institutions, and to all enterprises pertaining to the welfare of the public or the city.
>
> He was a generous friend to the poor, for whom he always had a warm heart and open hand, and who will sadly miss his constant interest in them. As a friend, he was unassuming, sincere, loyal and magnanimous, and as a husband and father, the kindliness of his disposition and his tender affection for those who were near and dear to him, was daily made manifest. The loss to the community of such a man is great, but to his friends and family it is irreparable.
>
> We tender our profound sympathy to the family in their bereavement, and ask that this memorial be spread upon the minutes, and a copy be sent to the family and the daily papers.

Moerlein Brewery workers honoring the memory of Christian Moerlein with a toast on the occasion of his death in 1897.

CHAPTER 4

Cincinnati's Beer Barons

Origins

MILLIONS OF GERMAN IMMIGRANTS came to America in the nineteenth century, with many finding their way to the Queen City of the West, where they filled up the area north of the Miami-Erie Canal, resulting in the creation of the German district known as Over-the-Rhine. Germans not only brought their trades, professions, customs, and traditions, but also a taste for the German-style of beer known as lager beer. Seizing the initiative, ambitious and enterprising Germans launched breweries in Over-the-Rhine, the nearby West End, and elsewhere to meet the demand, creating family run companies and even brewing empires, and emerged on the scene as a new type of entrepreneur—the German-American beer baron.

Cincinnati's beer barons believed in the American Dream and the notion that you could "make it" in America by means of hard work, thrift, and persistence. Many of the German immigrants were from Bavaria and involved their entire families in their brewing companies, with sons often studying at brewing academies in Germany and, as previously mentioned, daughters marrying members of other brewing-family dynasties.

While the beer barons were the founding fathers, their descendants carried on the German brewing heritage. American-born beer barons not only carried on, but embellished this heritage, such as George Moerlein, the son of Christian Moerlein, who rode into saloons on horseback up and down Vine Street, promoting Moerlein beer. Beer barons were often flashy and flamboyant showmen who had a knack for catching the public's attention.

Cincinnati's beer barons usually lived close to their breweries and were an integral part of the community, belonging to and supporting area churches and German societies and the festivals they sponsored, often helping organize events such as Saengerfest and German Day. They also gave back to the community-at-large in a host of philanthropic endeavors—for example, John Hauck's support of the Cincinnati Zoo, which enriched the social and cultural life of the city.[1]

The glowing accolades and songs of praise written in honor of Christian Moerlein should not be misconstrued to assume that he was something of a saint, other Cincinnati German beer barons were often described in similar fashion. As noted earlier, local histories, especially the so-called mug books, tended to present a positive portrait of the individuals they covered. However, as also noted, they had to ring true and stick to the facts in order to attain community-wide acceptance. In the case of Moerlein, for example, all of the biographies of him are in agreement with one another regarding what kind of person he was. Taken together, they help us reconstruct not only the image of Moerlein, but also of the man behind the image.

Cincinnati German Beer Barons

The biographies of other Cincinnati German beer barons reveal they were very much alike and they were portrayed in ways that closely resemble one another. For example, Charles F. Goss writes of Gottlieb Muhlhauser (1836–1905), who served as president of the Löwen-Brauerei/Lion Brewery,

Mr. Muhlhauser was essentially a self-made man and his success was due to those characteristic attributes of his German ancestry—honesty, energy, ambition, tenacity of purpose and other admirable qualities, which he possessed in a very marked degree. He was of a kind and genial disposition which won him the esteem and admiration of many friends, and the summing up of his life is most fittingly expressed in a set of resolutions passed by the Cincinnati Chamber of Commerce at his death and from which is extracted the following. . . . Mr. Muhlhauser had many good qualities—the prompt fulfillment of all obligations was to him an important duty; he was kind by nature, modest in deportment, warm in his sympathies and true to every trust. In his home life he was never so happy as when surrounded by members of his family, whom he dearly loved. . . . In his death, the Cincinnati Chamber of Commerce has lost one of its oldest and most valued members and the city of Cincinnati a true and enterprising citizen.[2]

The *History of Cincinnati and Hamilton County* (1894) says of John Hauck, president of the Hauck Brewing Company,

Mr. Hauck's position in the business world of Cincinnati is both enviable and prominent, and inasmuch as his success was solely due to his indefatigable efforts and his efficiency in his peculiar branch of trade, the German population of Cincinnati has just cause to take great pride in counting him among their number. Honorable political positions have frequently been offered him, but he has always refused, giving his exertions solely to his own business. He only accepted the presidency of the German National Bank, and the brilliant success of that institution during his connection with it showed the confidence which the business world reposed in him. Mr. Hauck has always stood ready to support enterprises of public interest, and indeed during his entire business career there has been no public enterprise of any consequence in which he did not take a prominent part.[3]

By going through the biographies of Moerlein, a long list of descriptive terms and phrases can be found. A representative sampling includes the following: industrious, untiringly energetic, of firm

THE WINDISCH MUHLHAUSER BREWING CO·

CINCINNATI. OHIO

LION BREWERY, Brewers and Bottlers of THE CELEBRATED LION BEER

Ohios Muster-Brauerei

Ihre Bestimmungen, Maschinerie und ihr Produkt haben den höchsten Punkt der Vollkommenheit erreicht und stehen ohne Konkurrenz da.

THE JOHN HAUCK BREWING Co.

Cincinnati, O.

Unsere Marken, Faß- und Flaschenbier:

„Golden Eagle", „Imperial".

„Special Dark",

gebraut von feinstem Malz und auserlesenstem Hopfen, übertreffen alle anderen Produkte dieser Art.

resolve, insightful, responsive, sociable, decisive, far-seeing, charitable, frugal, decent, modest, cordial, kindly, unassuming, sincere, loyal, magnanimous, and honest. Moreover, he was described as having an impeccable character, indomitable will, and was noted for his outstanding administrative skills, good judgment, integrity, and simplicity.

Such descriptors bring a picture of Christian Moerlein into sharp focus. They provide insight into the basic elements of his personality, as well as the kinds of attributes in his makeup that contributed to his phenomenal success. Taken together, they explain the growth and development of the Christian Moerlein Brewing Company, a family run company centered on the person of Christian Moerlein. They not only help us understand Moerlein, but other beer barons as well, since they shared many of the same kinds of character traits that are ascribed to him.

Appendix A includes the biographies of several other beer barons of the area together with a comparative analysis of them showing how much they resembled one another and how they were all "cut from the same cloth."

A National Phenomenon

Cincinnati's beer barons were certainly not unique, but rather much like those found elsewhere, but especially in Saint Louis and Milwaukee, the other two cities forming the German Triangle. In *Ambitious Brew: The Story of American Beer*, Maureen Ogle discusses the German immigrants who created the American brewing industry, noting that

> Historians generally scorn the idea of the "great man," but these émigrés who became the giants of the American brewing industry were made of rare and precious materials; were in their own way, great men who ranged through their days oblivious to indecision or failure, dismissive of doubts and human frailty. . . . Their personalities differed, but circumstances and a passion for competition linked their futures. . . .

Their breweries sat before them as lumps of clay, raw potential on which each man's ambition could work its will.[4]

Ogle finds that "Like the nation they adopted as home, these men were wedded to the future, not the past, and so entered their careers unburdened by stone-etched ideas about how a brewery ought to be run and who its customers should be." She also notes that the most successful brewery in the nation, the Anheuser-Busch, was, like many of the breweries of the Cincinnati beer barons, a family run affair: "For more than 150 years, the family has nurtured and built and fought, trusting almost no one but themselves to care as much about the company's name and its beer as they did."[5] The same story can be found in brewery after brewery in the history of German-American brewing.

Regarding Busch, Ogle writes that he "was a natural leader, thanks to what one friend described as 'assertiveness and good natured aggressiveness' and an optimistic arrogance rooted in intelligence, self-confidence, and charisma. . . . When he spoke, he hypnotized his audience with sweeping gestures." Writing of Frederick Pabst, Ogle notes that "Like Adolphus Busch, Pabst commanded any room he entered. But if Busch's charisma issued from his flamboyant self-assurance, Pabst flowed from quieter self-confidence, although he, like Busch, possessed a kind nature and generous warmth."[6]

Each had their own individual style and approach, but the similarity among them is striking. Together, they contributed to the emergence of the popular image of the beer baron.

Brewery District historical marker.

CHAPTER 5

The Old World

Family Origins

CHRISTIAN MOERLEIN WAS BORN IN THE VILLAGE OF TRUPPACH, which is located in the northern part of Bavaria in the region known as Oberfranken, or Upper Franconia. It is directly to the southwest of the city of Bayreuth, which is home of the famous opera house of composer Richard Wagner. According to Frederic Spotts, Franconia "is one of the loveliest corners of Germany—an area of charming towns, architectural gems and forest hills known as Franconian Switzerland."[1]

Wagner chose Bayreuth as the location for his *Festspielhaus* due to these factors, as well as the fact that it was roughly in the center of Germany. Because it was in Bavaria, Bayreuth enjoyed the protection of King Ludwig. Christian Moerlein, therefore, was born in a beautiful region that was centrally located in the German states, and one destined to play an important role in German cultural history.

The village of Truppach is a small village without a church or school, both of which are located in the nearby village of Mengersdorf. Both villages have been annexed and are now part of the town of Mistelgau. This part of Upper Franconia is predominantly Lutheran as was the Moerlein family. Archives of the Evangelical-Lutheran Church of Bavaria provide us with information on the historical origins of the family.[2]

According to church records, the Moerlein family can be traced back to Paulus Mörlein (1717–95). The original German spelling of the name is with an umlaut and is pronounced in German as *mur-lein*, whereas in the United States the name is spelled without an umlaut and with the addition of the letter "e." Also, the pronunciation has been Americanized as *more-lein*. Other variations of the name found in church records are Mehrlein, Meehrlein, Möhrlein, and Möhrlin.

Born in the village of Altenhann, which is near the city of Regensburg, Paulus Mörlein at some time moved to the city of Bayreuth, as the records list him as a mercenary soldier in the service of the margrave of Bayreuth. He was the eldest son of Paul Mörlein, a coach driver. Paulus became postmaster of Bayreuth, but at some time moved his place of residence to the nearby village of Truppach. His son, Johann Georg Mörlein (1756–1809), became a blacksmith there, the first in the history of the family. His only son, Conrad Mörlein (1793–1860), was the father of Christian.

Like his father before him, Conrad Mörlein was also a blacksmith. The church records refer to him more specifically as a *Huf- und Waffenschmied* (black- and gunsmith). This latter aspect of his trade might relate back to his grandfather having been a mercenary soldier. Also, it is interesting to note that in America the Moerleins were avid gun collectors, which probably relates to their family's black- and gunsmith background.

Conrad Mörlein married Margaretha Taut (1798–1875), the daughter of Johann Taut, a farmer in Wohnsgehaig. Christian (1818–97) was the oldest of four children. He had a sister Magdalena (1819) and brother Martin (1822) who died in infancy, and a brother Johann Georg (1824–82). Present-day descendants of the family derive from Christian's youngest brother, Johann Georg, and still reside in the area. The following entry can be found after Christian's name in the church records: "*Ausgewandert nach Amerika*" (Immigrated to America).

Sign to the village of Truppach.

Landscape around village of Truppach.

Aside from being a blacksmith, Christian's father is also listed in church records as *"Ortsvorsteher"* (mayor), thus indicating that the family occupied an honorable place in the community. His blacksmith shop and home was located in the most impressive building in town—the castle of Truppach. This large structure with four towers dates back to medieval times. Much of the original building was destroyed during the Reformation, but was then rebuilt. Records as to the ownership of the castle are now lost, but the family probably lived there since the mid-eighteenth century, when Paul Mörlein and family moved to Truppach from Bayreuth.

Moerlein's home in Truppach.

Bavaria

Up to the time of Napoleon, Franconia consisted of several principalities and was not a united state. The village of Truppach was part of the principality of Ansbach-Bayreuth, which had been ruled since the thirteenth century by landgraves who were members of the House of

Hohenzollern, the same family that reigned in Prussia. After the family died out in 1791, Ansbach-Bayreuth became a Prussian province, but Prussian rule came to an end as a result of the defeat of the Prussian Army by Napoleon's troops at the Battle of Jena in 1804. These and other military victories led to the demise of the Holy Roman Empire in 1806, causing the German states to be completely reorganized at the instigation of France.

Due to its support of Napoleon, Bavaria was raised by France from the status of a dukedom to that of a kingdom and it was able to acquire additional territory, including Franconia and with it Ansbach-Bayreuth. Although Franconians from then on were citizens of the Kingdom of Bavaria, they continued to maintain their regional identity as Franconians. Today, Bayreuth is a *Landkreis* (county) within Upper Franconia, one of the seven administrative districts in the state of Bavaria.

By the time of Moerlein's birth in 1818, Bavaria had just celebrated its twelfth year as a kingdom and Franconia its twelfth year as part of it. As a result of its newly found status, its ruler, Maximilian, assumed the title of king of Bavaria in 1806. In 1825 his son, Ludwig I, succeeded him on the throne, ruling until the time of the 1848 Revolution. During Moerlein's youth in Bavaria and until his immigration in 1841, Ludwig I served as head of state, and the political conditions of that time are worth noting as they relate to the reasons why Moerlein chose to immigrate to America.

Ludwig I (1786–1868) was the grandfather of the so-called "mad king" Ludwig II (1825–68), and was no less colorful and controversial than his grandson, who built the castle Neuschwanstein and supported composer Richard Wagner. Thanks to Ludwig I, the world's largest festival came into being. In 1810 he married Therese of Saxe-Hildburghausen and the annual celebration of their wedding anniversary laid the foundation of what has become known as Oktoberfest.

Like his grandson, Ludwig I was a patron of the arts and also promoted the industrialization of Bavaria. Unfortunately, he became ever more autocratic and oppressive as time went on. This and the widespread disgust with his numerous affairs contributed ultimately to his downfall during the 1848 Revolution, forcing him to abdicate. The revolution itself was the end result of long-standing discontent with the prevalent political status quo in the German states, going back to the end of the Napoleonic era, but in Bavaria, Ludwig I was also a causative factor.

Political discontent in the German states had led to the emergence of student organizations known as the *Burschenschaften*. In 1817, they called for a national convention at the castle called the Wartburg, where Luther had translated the Bible into German. There they protested political conditions and proclaimed their support of German unity.[3]

Prince Klemens von Metternich, the Austrian chancellor, together with the Friedrich Wilhelm II, king of Prussia, pushed a set of oppressive measures through the parliament of the German Confederation known as the Karlsbad Decrees, resulting in the censorship of the press and tighter control of educational institutions. This also stifled the parliaments of the various German states, which met mainly behind closed doors, and whose proceedings were not reported on in the press.

A series of harsh winters and poor harvests, especially in southwestern Germany, had led to an impoverished peasantry, which in many areas hovered barely above the subsistence level. These political and economic conditions combined to make for increasing discontent in the German states. In terms of religious conditions in a predominantly Catholic state such as Bavaria, the church was under the supervision of the king, who had the authority to appoint bishops and other church positions.

The revolution of 1830 in France triggered the revolution of 1832 in Germany, which began with the protest demonstration known as the Hambach Fest. This led to a number of revolutionary outbursts across the German states, followed by an even greater degree of political suppression and oppression. In accordance with the spirit of the time, Ludwig I increasingly endorsed a reactionary course of action, which found expression in law by means of the Bavarian parliament.

Given these conditions throughout the German states, it is not surprising that a major revolution, the 1848 Revolution, spread like wildfire throughout the German states of Europe, and in Bavaria led to Ludwig I's abdication in favor of his son, Maximilian (1811–64). The last straw had been his many scandalous affairs, especially his liaison with his Irish-born mistress Lola Montez (Eliza Gilbert).[4]

By the time of his immigration in 1841, Moerlein had already experienced the greater part of his life in Bavaria under the reign of Ludwig I. Given the conditions there, as well as elsewhere in the German states, it is not surprising that German immigration to America was increasing dramatically, but the point has to be kept in mind that Moerlein was a citizen of the Kingdom of Bavaria, so conditions there are of particular importance as regard to his immigration.

Emigration Motives

Aside from these general factors motivating emigration from Bavaria and which most likely also influenced Christian Moerlein, the biographies of him, which we have discussed thus far, stress his desire to become independent and establish a household of his own. For example, Charles F. Goss notes,

> He was anxious to marry and establish a home of his own but he could not afford to with such a meager income. It was this that awakened in him the desire to go to America where better business opportunities could be secured, and in this emergency his father offered him forty dollars. With this as his sole capital he started for Bremen, walking the entire distance. He carried a kit of tools and worked by the way in order to save his money. At length the distance between his old home and the seaport town—three hundred miles—was covered and at Bremen he embarked on the sailing vessel *Rebecca*, which after a voyage of fifty-eight days reached the harbor of Baltimore.[5]

At the time of his emigration, Moerlein was twenty-three years old, so the question might be asked about military service, as this factor played a role in causing many to immigrate to the United States. In the Kingdom of Bavaria one was subject to military service for the two years following the January after one's twenty-first birthday and the required time for military service was rather lengthy—six years. During peacetime, individuals were selected by means of a lottery. For Moerlein, this meant that he was eligible for conscription from 1 January 1839 to 1 January 1841.

Since Moerlein immigrated in mid-1841, it is clear that his number had not been called, as he would have otherwise been in the Bavarian army until 1845 or 1847, depending on when his number might have been called. Due to the date of his immigration, it appears that he waited until after his period of eligibility had elapsed and then made the decision to immigrate. Had his number been called, chances are that he might not have come to America, but rather served his tour of duty and then returned back home to Truppach. It appears that after not getting drafted, he must have taken stock of his options for the future. What prospect did the future hold for him?

Church records list Moerlein as a blacksmith and beer brewer, which indicates that he had completed apprenticeship and journey-man years for both, as one would have to have certification to be listed for both of these trades. His biography indicates that from age eighteen to twenty-three he had been occupied with the *Wanderjahre* (journeyman years) that follow the earlier years of *Lehrjahre* (years of apprenticeship) of learning a trade with a master craftsman. The apprenticeship system relates to the dual track educational system in Germany, with one being vocational and the other academic.

Those taking the vocational track via the apprenticeship system ended up by becoming a *Meister* in their chosen vocation, in essence earning a master's degree in that area, just as one earns an academic degree in a given subject area. Indeed, one receives a *Meisterbrief* (master craftsman's diploma) on completion of one's years of apprenticeship and journeyman years. The usual number of journeyman years is three, but Moerlein spent five years, as he earned the necessary time to qualify for two trades: blacksmithing and brewing. As a result, Moerlein was now certified to engage in both trades.

During the following Wanderjahre, he would have traveled from place to place, working with various craftsmen, registering his stay with them in a *Wanderbuch* (journeyman's book). We do not know where Moerlein traveled during this time period, but journeymen were required to spend time in their homeland, so Moerlein's journeyman years would have been in Upper Franconia and included stays in nearby towns and villages, most likely also in the nearby city of Bayreuth.

These years might have opened up his eyes to the prospects of becoming a blacksmith or brewer. The former probably have meant working with his father at his blacksmith business and the latter working with his uncle at his brewery. His biographies indicate his desire to become independent and that the earnings would have been insufficient to establish a household. Given these circumstances, the only other real option on the horizon was emigration.

By now, he had already gone through his Wanderjahre, had traveled throughout the region, and had broadened his horizons. Now he would have to venture further afield and become an *Auswanderer* (emigrant). And with the vocational training he had behind him by this time, he no doubt felt well equipped to make his way in the New World.

An additional and more subtle motivational factor that might come into play is the Protestant work ethic, which played an important role in the rise of capitalism in general and in Europe in particular. This work ethic stresses the importance of an individual's vocational calling in life and the need to excel in it by means of hard work and persistence. These are exactly the kinds of virtues that defined Moerlein's life and were often used to describe him.

Moerlein came from a Lutheran region and family and once in Cincinnati he became a strong supporter of his church—there can be little doubt that he took his religious faith seriously. We might, therefore, conclude that the origins of his drive to succeed in life most likely derive from the Protestant work ethic, something which had its origins in the Lutheran Reformation.[6]

Auswanderung (Emigration)

Being the ambitious and enterprising young man that he was, Moerlein chose the emigration option. At the same time he was probably mulling over these thoughts, German emigration was definitely on the upswing and was a major topic of the day. His immigration to America, therefore, was certainly not unique, but rather part of this mass migration movement of the nineteenth century. Many others were motivated to immigrate by the same or similar factors that caused Moerlein to seek his luck in America, *das Land der unbegrenzten Möglichkeiten* (the land of unlimited possibilities). In the 1830s, German immigration numbered 124,726 and, in the 1840s, 385,434. By the 1850s, this number had risen to 976,072.[7]

By the time Moerlein emigrated, there was already a wealth of literature about America, most important of which was a book published in 1829 by Gottfried Duden. Entitled *Bericht über eine Reise nach den westlichen Staaten Nordamerikas*, Duden painted a glowing picture of America and the possibilities there for German immigrants. Considered the single most influential book about America in the history of German immigration, the book described Duden's travels, including vivid descriptions of Cincinnati, as well as the Ohio Valley. He wrote of Cincinnati: "Cincinnati is called the most beautiful city of the entire West, and truly the European who involuntarily associates all kinds of ideas about savage life with the words American interior, could scarcely trust his eyes if he could suddenly be transported from his home to this city."[8] Although it is unknown if Moerlein knew of Duden's book, we do know that it influenced many to come to America, including to Cincinnati. And even if he had not read the book, its mere publication reflects the interest in America in the German states.[9]

Another motivational factor for causing Germans to think about immigration was that the richest man in America in the early nineteenth century was a German immigrant: John Jacob Astor (1763–1848). Gustav Koerner called him "the prince of trade and commerce."[10] His American Fur Company developed into a worldwide business and Astor acquired extensive land holdings, both of which made him extremely wealthy. In the process, Astor emerged as the archetype of what became known as "the self-made man," an individual who had basically risen by means of grit and determination from "rags to riches." German immigrants saw in him a vision of what they too might also become.

For those interested in the Ohio Valley region there were also two well-known German immigrant success stories: Major David Ziegler (1748–1811) and Martin Baum (1765–1831). Ziegler had served in the Continental Army during the American Revolution and thereafter continued service in the U.S. Army and was stationed at Fort Washington in Cincinnati. After his retirement from the service, he served as the first mayor of Cincinnati (1802) and then held several other public offices.

In Cincinnati Baum established the Miami Exporting Company and a whole array of other businesses, making him the wealthiest man in the region. And by organizing the stream of German immigrants to come to the area to work in his various companies, he became known as the founding father of the German immigration to Cincinnati and the Ohio Valley and also served as an early mayor of Cincinnati. Ziegler and Baum both provided additional success stories that replicated the national success story of Astor.[11] They all worked together to provide a powerful elixir to prospective German immigrants of what they might attain in the New World.

CHAPTER 6

The New World

Over-the-Rhine

IN COMING TO AMERICA Moerlein did not head directly to Cincinnati, but rather found his way there after having been in the country for three-quarters of a year. He arrived at the port of Baltimore on 23 June 1841, but did not arrive in Cincinnati until the following year on 1 April 1842. After his arrival, his travels in search of work took him to Pittsburgh, Pennsylvania; Wheeling, (West) Virginia; Portsmouth, Ohio; Hendricksburg, Ohio; and, then back to Wheeling. From there he moved to Cincinnati, Ohio. No reference is made to family connections in any of these places, but he did have friends in Portsmouth, Ohio.

Moerlein probably learned of Cincinnati from his friends and may have been advised to seek out the Over-the-Rhine district, where Germans had already begun to congregate. Located north of the central business district, Over-the-Rhine was the obvious destination for Moerlein. The borders of this predominantly German district were defined by the Miami-Erie Canal, completed in 1831. Locally the barge canal had been dubbed as the "Rhine" since when one crossed over it, one entered the German district.[1]

Cincinnati in 1845.

In Over-the-Rhine Moerlein would have found a growing German community with German bakeries, meat markets, stores, churches, newspapers, etc. It was an ideal place for him to settle down, get established, and eventually set up his brewery. In terms of marketing strategy he was in the best place for getting a brewery going, surrounded as he was with a population that would most likely be interested in his product. Carl Wittke provides us with the following portrait of the district:

> Cincinnati's German community, in its early years, was concentrated largely in the area north of where the canal entered the city, and was known as "Over-the-Rhine." Here the Germans lived in neat little frame and brick houses built flush with the sidewalk, and with backyards fenced in with lattice work and planted with flower and vegetable gardens. Every Saturday, German housewives scrubbed the front steps of their homes until they were snow white. Here the German Hausfrau nourished her family with German food and delicacies which quickly became part of the American culinary art. After working hours and on Sunday, the men sought recreation in the taverns, played euchre, skat and pinochle, or brought their families to the beer gardens to listen to old familiar German airs.[2]

Over-the-Rhine beer garden.

German immigrants pouring into the Over-the-Rhine district and environs came from a variety of places in Europe. According to the U.S. Census and other reports, German immigration predominated from northwestern Germany, especially from Hannover, Oldenburg, and Prussia. The next largest number came from southern Germany, especially the Swabians and Bavarians. And the third largest number of German immigrants came from other areas, especially Austro-Hungary.

The largest of these groups was the first group from northwestern Germany. Among other things, the northwestern Germans contributed a food item that is popular throughout the area—Goetta, which is Low German for the High German word *Grützewurst*. North Germans also were responsible for creating another well-known German neighborhood in Cincinnati called Wooden Shoe Hollow due to the fact that farmers and gardeners there wore wooden shoes just like in northern Germany.[3]

By 1840 the German-born population stood at 7 percent of a total population of about 50,000, but by 1850 had grown to 20 percent of a total population of 115,000. And, by 1870, the German stock (the German-born and the first generation American-born population) consisted of 34 percent of a total population of 215,000. By 1890 the German stock had reached a total of 58 percent of the total population of about 300,000. In the course of a century, the population of German ancestry had, therefore, grown from the status of being a minority group to become the majority ethnic ancestry group in the region, influencing just about everything in the region.[4]

Given the large German element in Cincinnati, it is no wonder that Moerlein settled down on Elm Street in the Over-the-Rhine district. Shrewdly sensing the market potential, he eventually established his highly successful brewery. It all must have made perfect sense to him. It would take only a little more than a decade after his arrival in 1842 to get a brewery up and running. And the entire region was well suited for it as well.

Historian Henry Howe provides us with a glimpse of what the area as a whole looked like in the 1840s when Moerlein arrived there.

> This city [Cincinnati] is near the eastern extremity of a valley about twelve miles in circumference, surrounded by beautiful hills, which rise to the height of 300 feet by gentle and varying slopes, and mostly covered with native forest trees. The summit of these hills presents a beautiful and picturesque view of the city and valley. The city is built on two table-lands, the one elevated from forty to sixty feet above the other. . . . The population in 1800 was 750; in 1810, 2,540; in 1820, 9,602; in 1830, 24,831; and, in 1840, 46,338; and, in 1847, over 90,000. . . . Covington and Newport, opposite in Kentucky, and Fulton and, the adjacent parts of Mill Creek Township on the north are, in fact suburbs of Cincinnati, and if added to the above

population would extend to 105,000. . . . The inhabitants are from every State in the Union, and from various countries in Europe. . . . Nearly one-fifth of the adult population is Germans. But England, Ireland, Scotland, France, and Wales have furnished considerable numbers.[5]

Howe also goes on to describe the thriving business and industry of the area as follows:

Cincinnati is an extensive manufacturing place. . . . The manufactures of the city, already large, may be expected to greatly increase. By a late enumeration, it appears that the manufacturers of Cincinnati of all kinds of employ 10,647 persons, a capital of $14,541,842, and produce articles of over seventeen million dollars of value. . . . The trade of Cincinnati embraces the country from the Ohio to the lakes, north and south; and from the Scioto to the Wabash, east and west. The Ohio River lines in Kentucky, for fifty miles down, and as far up as the Virginia line, make their purchases here. Its manufactures are sent into the upper and lower Mississippi country. . . . Cincinnati enjoys great facilities for communication with the surrounding country. The total length of canals, railroads and turnpikes which centre here, completed and constructing, is 1,125 miles. Those who have made it a matter of investigation predict that Cincinnati will eventually be a city of a very great population.[6]

Howe also cites one exuberant author, J. W. Scott, who predicted in 1841 "that in one hundred years from this time, Cincinnati will be the greatest city in America; and by the year of our Lord 2000 the greatest city in the world." Howe also notes that he did not "have the space to recapitulate the arguments on which this prediction is based. The prediction itself we place on record for future reference."[7] Although Cincinnati, of course, did not rise to such expectations, it certainly did become the largest city along the Ohio River and such predictions reflect the burgeoning enthusiasm for the area in the nineteenth century. The appeal of the area even gave rise to Henry Wadsworth Longfellow's charming toast to Cincinnati in one of his poems.

To the Queen of the West,
In her garlands dressed,
On the banks of the Beautiful River.[8]

The Miami-Erie Canal was better known as the "Rhine."

CHAPTER 7

The Soul of the Company

The Heir Apparent

HAVING OUTLINED SOME IMPORTANT HISTORICAL BACKGROUND, we can now return to the subject of our study—Christian Moerlein. As previously noted, a key element in the success of the Moerlein Brewing Company was that it was a family run business with Christian Moerlein at the helm. Moreover, it also had the trappings of a dynasty, which had established a brewing empire in Over-the-Rhine. As "king of the industry" Moerlein no doubt viewed eldest son George not only as the rising star on the horizon, but also as the crown prince who, in time, would accede to the throne and take his place as Cincinnati's beer baron Over-the-Rhine.

Building on the foundations established by his enterprising father, George became the most colorful and flamboyant member of the Moerlein family, and was widely viewed as the heir apparent to the Moerlein Brewing Company. Had it not been for his untimely death six years prior to the demise of his father, George might have led the brewery business up to the time of Prohibition.

However, before his death he had accomplished a great deal, being essentially responsible for making the Moerlein brand well known nationally. He also published a travel narrative of his worldwide travels, which is a collector's item today. Above all, he was a masterful showman, who took an active role in community affairs. Just as Buffalo Bill helped create the enduring image we have today of the Wild West, so too did George Moerlein put his own unique stamp on the emerging image of the beer baron. Both myths developed at roughly the same time and helped explain the changes that were transforming American society from its frontier past to its increasingly urban present and future.

George Moerlein

A Cincinnati German history, *Cincinnati und sein Deutschthum* (1901), observed that "It is a noble feeling to gaze at the long list of outstanding German-Americans, who have contributed to making Cincinnati what it is today. Few of them, however, have exerted such a lasting impact as did George Moerlein, whose passing on 31 August 1891 amounted to an irretrievable loss for the entire city of Cincinnati."[1] There is no question that his passing was a great loss for the Moerlein Brewing Company, as well as the region due to his wide-ranging social, cultural, and political activities and influences in the area.

George Moerlein was born 8 June 1852 in the wood-frame home of the Moerlein family located on Elm Street, where the malt house was later built. After attending public school and Woodward High School, he decided to prepare himself for the brewing trade in Germany, and began his studies in 1869 at the Brewing Academy in Nuremberg.[2] Shortly thereafter, however, the Franco-Prussian War broke out. So enthusiastic was he with the German cause that he requested and received special permission to accompany German forces to the front lines.

After witnessing the war firsthand that led to the unification of Germany under the leadership of Chancellor Otto von Bismarck, George returned to Nuremberg with the victorious Bavarian troops who had fought in the conflict.[3] After completing his studies and graduating with high marks, he returned to Cincinnati to take a position as business manager of the Moerlein Brewing Company. Known for his attention to detail, he swiftly climbed the hierarchical ladder of the company.

In 1876 he was responsible for representing the company at the Centennial Exposition in Philadelphia, and masterfully introduced beer from the Moerlein Brewing Company to the East. Ever the great showman, George Moerlein presented a pavilion in the Agriculture Hall that mesmerized visitors. Considered bedazzling by all who viewed it, the pavilion displayed twelve life-sized figures that represented the seasons, the continents, and historical and symbolic figures. For example, Columbia and Pocahontas represented America, and there was also "a full-sized statue of a horse bearing a life-sized image of 'the standard bearer of the famous Bismarck regiment' reared up from the roof." Moreover, these figures as well as the pyramids of Moerlein beer bottles surrounding them "rotated, thanks to a two-horsepower engine hidden beneath the works. The more dignified horse and rider remained stationary."[4] This was not only a great spectacle, it generated a tremendous amount of publicity and George Moerlein had orchestrated it all with precision. The brewery was now definitely on the national map as far as brewing was concerned and George Moerlein had put it there.

The 1876 Exposition transformed the growing brewery from a regionally known company to a nationally known one. Business advanced so much that it proved more than it could handle. For this reason, a stock company was formed on 15 September 1881, with a capital of a million dollars, a sizable sum for the time. George was elected as vice president of the brewery, with his father, Christian, serving as president. The officers of the Christian Moerlein Company consisted of members of the family, clearly demonstrating that this was a family run business.

President — Christian Moerlein
Vice President — George Moerlein
Secretary — John Goetz, Jr. (Christian's son-in-law)
Treasurer — Jacob Moerlein
General Superintendent — John Moerlein

According to *Cincinnati und sein Deutschthum*, "George Moerlein was the soul of the company, and the colossal upswing that the brewery experienced was due to his enterprising spirit, intelligence and energy."[5] This was reflected in the increased sales of Moerlein beer as the following statistics of the number of barrels of beer produced clearly indicates:

1880	–	100,000
1883	–	114,276
1885	–	153,822
1887	–	192,849
1890	–	225,000
1895	–	500,000

In short, the sale of Moerlein beer doubled in the 1880s, an amazing growth rate. In 1866, the company produced 25,000 barrels of beer, but by 1890 was producing ten times that number—a phenomenal 225,000 barrels. By 1895 the company doubled sales of that produced in 1890, again, a phenomenal rate of growth and development for the company. According to William L. Downard, George Moerlein "was primarily responsible for this shift in market orientation. He had become general manager in 1872 at the age of twenty, but rapidly displayed business acumen of a mature entrepreneur."[6]

George was also involved with other business endeavors, including the Southern Granite Company, which he owned, and which provided materials for a variety of purposes, including for the street construction in the Greater Cincinnati area. Moerlein was also active in the social, cultural, and political life of the community. He founded the Elm Street Club, and belonged to the Lincoln and Blaine Clubs, the Odd Fellows, and many other German societies. Although he never held political office, George Moerlein exerted a great deal of political clout in the Republican Party, and before his death led the wing of the party that opposed the man who controlled it—George B. Cox, better known as Boss Cox.[7]

George Moerlein's gravesite at Spring Grove Cemetery.

CHAPTER 8

Showman Par Excellence

George Moerlein's Travels Abroad

DURING 1884/85, GEORGE MOERLEIN TOOK A TRIP around the world and then published a book about his travels.[1] A reviewer of George Moerlein's subsequent travel narrative noted that "conversation stamps him as a deep thinker and an earnest student . . . it is a pleasure to see a busy, brainy man like Mr. Moerlein, who in spite of tremendous business can still find time for scholarly pursuits."[2]

In 1886, M. & R. Burgheim of Cincinnati published his travel account in English and German editions as *A Trip Around the World* and *Eine Reise um die Welt*. In 1887 another printing of the German edition appeared with the title page in color. Beautifully bound in red buckram with black and gold letters, the volume is adorned with gilt edged pagination and contains 110 lithographic illustrations, printed in oil colors by the Krebs Lithographing Company of Cincinnati.

Moerlein noted in the introduction that "The illustrations were carefully chosen from a collection of over eight hundred original pictures gathered during our travels, and are colored true to nature." And, he observed that the Krebs Company "secured the ablest artists

Title page of the English-language edition of George Moerlein's book.

and spared neither pains nor expense."[3] Its fine binding, lettering, and gilt-edge pages, together with numerous colored lithographs, make Moerlein's travel book a highly sought-after item on the antiquarian book market today, often fetching increasingly high prices.

Title page of the German-language edition of George Moerlein's book.

A Trip Around the World

The 205-page book provides a fascinating account of Moerlein's worldwide adventure that he began in November 1884. In his introduction he wrote,

> Late in the fall of 1884, I was busily occupied one Sunday afternoon, in studying an atlas for the purpose of informing myself as to the different railroad lines to the Pacific coast, to which section of the country I contemplated making a trip for the double purpose of viewing the scenery and improving my health.
>
> While thus engaged, the idea suddenly dawned upon my mind that the time had arrived for me to undertake a long cherished journey—to make a trip around the world.
>
> After careful consideration I determined that, providing my parents consented and a suitable companion could be found, I would hazard it. That very evening I unfolded my scheme at a family meeting.
>
> At the outstart, no one would listen to my propositions, but after several days of importuning and reasoning, pleading and pledging, I succeeded in satisfying all that the journey would greatly benefit me both mentally and physically.
>
> I was not long in persuading two of my oldest and dearest friends, Mr. Charles Cramer and Mr. John F. Leidlein, to accompany me on the proposed tour. We wasted no time in getting ready, for in just ten days after I reached my conclusion, we started, prepared to see and learn.[4]

Ever the astute publicist, George kept in touch with the local press. He noted that he sent letters from time to time to two Cincinnati newspapers, the *Commercial Gazette* and the *Volksblatt*, which published his letters as a series of travel articles. Later on, he decided to collect them and other writings and publish them. "At the solicitation of a number of friends, who expressed a desire to have these letters and a brief account of our travels in convenient form, I decided to have this book published." He also commented that "The letters have been somewhat changed in order that I might introduce incidents, events and facts overlooked then."[5]

Moerlein began his book as follows: "On the evening of the 8th of November, 1884, our party, escorted by a number of intimate friends started for the depot. The customary farewells and hopes for a 'happy journey and safe return' were exchanged, and in a few minutes we were speeding across the country on an Ohio and Mississippi train. Thus was commenced our journey around the world."[6] In a series of seventeen chapters Moerlein proceeds to provide a vivid account of his travel experiences, noting that a total of 35,194 miles were covered altogether.

From Vienna to Cincinnati

Moerlein indicated that his focus was on the Far East, noting, "I have confined myself almost entirely to the countries of the 'Far East,' because it was there we sojourned longest and had the opportunity of closely viewing the many, to us strange sights and scenes."[7] Although he focuses mainly on the Far East, in the final chapter of his book, Moerlein devoted the last few pages to discussion of his journey from Vienna back to Cincinnati. Here he writes,

From *A Trip Around the World*
by George Moerlein

Moving on in our final tour through Europe, which consumed five weeks, we traveled from Vienna to Munich, from there to Strassburg, and then to Bischweiler in Alsace. In the last-named city we met with the most cordial reception at the hands of the Rinkenberger family, to whom we had letters of introduction from several members of that family, who have located in America and are intimate friends of ours. We had originally intended to make our stay two days, but prolonged the visit to six. Every morning there was some new surprise in store for us. Each one [vying] with the others in showing us attentions. Our entertainment could not have been more generous.

A large hunting-wagon was at our disposal, in which we made delightful excursions into the surrounding country and along the banks of the beautiful and romantic river Rhine. No pains were spared by these friends to make our visit pleasant and they succeeded admirably. It was with no little regret that we bade these kind people farewell and resumed our journey.

From Bischweiler we journeyed to Mayence, from there to Frankfort-on-the-Main, and then back to Mayence again. Almost one whole day, from morning until evening was spent on the Rhine in reaching Cologne from Mayence. A delightful May day, combined with the famous Rhenish scenery, made the trip one long to be remembered. From Cologne we traveled to Berlin, thence to Dresden, Bayreuth, and Nuremberg. At Nuremberg we spent the time gloriously in the company and under the direction of my dear friends Ferdinand Carl, the proprietor and editor of the *Hopfenzeitung*, the official organ of the extensive hop trade of the continent of Europe, P. Marlier, J. Hoffner, and Hans Bauriedel, three successful businessmen.[8] They had been my most intimate associates during the years 1869, 1870, 1871, when I attended school in that city. This was our first meeting since the fall of 1871. After a separation of fourteen years the re-union was indeed a happy one.[9]

Events and escapades of days gone by were recalled and related to the enjoyment of my traveling companions. Our parting was truly painful, and we all fervently wished for another meeting in the near future.

From Nuremberg our course lay to Stuttgart, Carlsruhe, Strassburg, Paris, London, and Liverpool. In all cities mentioned we stopped over long enough to obtain a correct idea of their appearance and also view many of the interesting sights for which they are noted. But so much has been written of these European cities by the hundreds of travelers who yearly visit them, that I deem it wholly unnecessary to enter upon a detailed account, and they are therefore passed with only a mention, so that the continuity of our trip might not be broken.

On June 20th we embarked from Liverpool on the finest and fleetest of all ocean steamers, the so-far invincible "Etruria." A dense fog which we encountered after we had covered about one-half of the distance across the Atlantic in extraordinary fast time, prevented us from making the customary quick passage for which the steamer has become famous. We steamed into the harbor of New York after the ninth day out. When the custom house officials boarded the steamer they had with them a party of friends from Cincinnati, who had come to New York as a reception committee. They were Messrs. August Wittgenfeld, Frank Tucker, Frank Rattermann, and John Moerlein.[10] Our greeting was warm and hearty; and our feelings at again grasping the hands of old friends, and seeing their familiar faces after such a journey "around the world," can readily be imagined.

After a short rest in New York we started on July 1st, at four o'clock in the afternoon and arrived the following afternoon at the Little Miami depot in Cincinnati, where a host of relatives and friends were on hand to meet us. After the usual handshakings and congratulations we hastened to the sacred family circle, there to discuss and relate our adventures. Thus ended our journey. We had accomplished our task without serious mishap or misfortune, not only benefited physically, but with our minds improved, and altogether well satisfied with the successful ending of our "Trip around the World."[11]

A review in the *Atlantic Monthly* (1887) made the following critical comments regarding Moerlein's book, noting that the illustrations were more colorful than the text:

> This book is singular among the books of the season for its reliance on illustrations printed in oil-colors. There are 110 of these, occupying pages by themselves, singly or in groups. They certainly afford a variety to the eye sated with the refinements of wood-engraving. The text is mainly from newspaper letters, written by the author when on his tour. He writes in a plain, unimaginative style, not so highly colored as his pictures.[12]

A Trip Around the World reflects the fact that George Moerlein was not only an author, but also a clever publicist as well, with his ongoing correspondence with the German- and English-language press of Cincinnati. He had studied brewing in Germany, had risen up the ranks in the Moerlein Brewing Company, and proven himself to be a master of the art of public relations.

Businessman and Showman Par Excellence

The flamboyant nature of George Moerlein was best described by Frank Grayson, who provides a vivid portrait of how he rode down Vine Street on horse, creating not only a dashing spectacle, but also publicity for the Moerlein Brewing Company.

> [E]verybody knew George and liked him. In addition, there was a fascination about the name of Moerlein. It carried an appeal that was irresistible. Well, anyhow, Mr. Moerlein drew up in front of Harff & Cramer's. He wheeled his horse and rode straight through the doorway. The thud of the horse's hoofs on the floor of the café startled its habitués out of their usual philosophical repose. Mr. Moerlein urged the horse forward, rode the length of the bar room, wheeled, rode back and stopped in front of the bar. He called for a glass of his own product, which he quaffed without taking his feet out of the stirrups. Then he rode out of the front door and cantered south on Vine Street. It was an unusual stunt. It brightened an otherwise dull afternoon for the rounders.[13]

Upon returning to Cincinnati from his world tour, George married Carrie Werner (1885), but there were no children to the relatively brief marriage. Since the 1870s, he had contributed to the tremendous upswing of the brewery, so that his death in 1891, which was due to inflammatory rheumatism, was a great loss to the Moerlein family and company.

The *Cincinnati Volksblatt* praised him in an obituary, noting that "The death of George Moerlein is not only a great loss for his family, but also for the entire city." It noted, "The exceptional intelligence of the deceased enabled him to preserve one of the greatest industrial establishments of the area and to advance it to an even greater reputation as well." It stressed that he was "a worthy representative of the noble traits that characterized the Moerlein family" and which included support for philanthropic causes on behalf of the community. And, it noted that there was hardly a charity, or worthy cause in the city that he had not contributed to, and, moreover, not with small, but sizable contributions.[14]

George Moerlein was not only a great businessman, but also a flamboyant showman, who loved adventure and travel. He contributed significantly to the growth and development of the Moerlein Brewing Company, as well as to the formation of the emerging image of the flashy and colorful beer baron. The unexpected demise of the heir apparent was, therefore, keenly felt. He had been "the soul of the company" and was a showman par excellence. Now he was gone, but the show had to go on.

CHAPTER 9

The Golden Age

Beer Baron at the Helm

THE YEAR 1891 MUST HAVE BEEN A HARD YEAR for Christian Moerlein. He had come to America fifty years earlier in 1841 with dreams of a better life and attained the American Dream for himself and his family. He had built the Moerlein Brewing Company from ground up with the help of his large family in the Over-the-Rhine district. But now his eldest son George was gone. It was an untimely loss for Moerlein, now age seventy-three. But he had faced hard knocks before, such as the loss of his first wife, Sophie, to the cholera epidemic. He had forged on and dealt with adversities in the past and would do so now again. At an age when most people pass the torch on to others, he had to continue on as the torchbearer. He had to—he was Christian Moerlein, "the king of the industry."

Fortunately, the Moerlein family was there to back him up. The executive board of the company was reorganized along family lines. Founding father Christian continued on as president, while son John moved up to the position of vice president.

President – Christian Moerlein
Vice President – John Moerlein
Second Vice President – John Goetz, Jr.
Treasurer – Jacob Moerlein
Secretary – Wilhelm Moerlein

Thanks to the leadership skills of Christian Moerlein and the strong support of the Moerlein family, the brewing business moved on with continued success as production steadily increased. Indeed, the time period from the 1890s down to the onset of Prohibition might be called the Golden Age of the Christian Moerlein Brewing Company. However, the foundations had been laid by Christian Moerlein and his son George. The brewery was now the largest in Cincinnati, in the state of Ohio and also one of the five largest in the United States.

This Golden Age of the Christian Moerlein Brewing Company, and of all brewing companies, came to an abrupt end, beginning with the harsh times of World War I, which brought with it anti-German sentiment and hysteria, followed by the passage of the Volstead Act to enforce Prohibition across the country. Such a turn of events, of course, could not have been foreseen in the 1890s, with the immediate focus at that time being the reorganization of the company's management team.

By the 1890s, the company was brewing the following varieties of beer:

Barbarossa
Culmbacher
Doppel
National Export
Old Jug Lager, also known as Old Krug
Wiener

National Export was especially noteworthy as it was advertised on the pottery jugs in which it was held as "Exhilarating, wholesome, stimulating, delicious, rejuvenating, & pure." What more could be asked for from a beer from the Moerlein Brewing Company? It was not only great beer, but was also good for your health, and almost

sounded like it had medicinal value. Therefore, one would have to assume that it was more than advisable to consume for one's health. An advertisement in the *Cincinnati Enquirer* (12 May 1889) even featured a bottle of National Export with the label carrying the following poem:

> The Moerlein "National Export" beer,
> Par excellence stands without a peer,
> From native shores to foreign lands,
> It heads the list of beverage brands,
> The convalescent, sick and well,
> The gay dun dine, the natty swell
> The scions of nobility,
> The peasant the king,
> Its songs of praise to sing,
> From Greenland's icy mountains,
> To India's burning strand,
> The native and the travelers,
> Drink "National Export" brand,
> A congress of all nations,
> Mid round and lusty cheers,
> Has crowned the "National Export,"
> The "Queen" of table beers.

What other beer could lay claim to having a poem written about it? And what other beer could be called "the Queen" of beers? It was the Queen of beers from the Queen City of the West that was appropriately named National Export, as it had a national reputation. No longer merely a regional brewery, the Christian Moerlein Brewing Company was by this time well situated as a brewery with national stature.

Cincinnati's Brewing Industry

The importance of the brewing industry for Cincinnati is underscored by the following passage:

Bottle of Jug Lager

From *History of Cincinnati and Hamilton County*, 1894

Cincinnati is one of the great brewing centers of the continent. Its peculiarly eligible location makes it possible to successfully meet the competition of other brewing centers, and as a distributing point it is unexcelled. To Mr. Shaw, of the Board of Trade, and industrial articles, published in the *Commercial Gazette*, we are indebted for a vast array of "facts and figures" relating to this colossal industry, the material portions of which are condensed and given herewith. The thirty-two breweries in and about Cincinnati pay the United States revenue department for stamps yearly nearly a million and a half of dollars. The local brewers are thoroughly up to date in all the improvements in the line of their business, and as a result, their products find a market not alone in every State of the Union, but in Canada, Mexico, South America, China, Japan and far away Australia. The export beer of Cincinnati has achieved a high-class reputation all over the world, and has made serious inroads into the export trade of Germany.

The Cincinnati brewers fear no competition; because the excellence and fame of their brews create a demand for them even in cities whose brewers have a greater aggregate capital invested. The trade has increased steadily, and all plants been enlarged and improved to meet the demand. There is not a brewery in this city and vicinity to-day whose plant is adequate to the demand for its product. Twenty years ago the aggregate output of the breweries here scarcely amounted to a half million barrels. In 1891–92 the aggregate output was 1,350,865 barrels, which record will this year be greatly increased. In 1872–73 the shipments of beer from Cincinnati breweries aggregated only 123,625 barrels; in 1891–92, 600,000 barrels were shipped. This shows the enormous growth of the brewing industry of Cincinnati, a growth which is being maintained despite the competition from all sides.

The local consumption of beer and ale is big enough to consume the product of many breweries, being last year some 815,000 barrels, representing 22,265,000 gallons, or an average of fifty gallons per capita for a population of 500,000. The amount paid by local consumers was approximately $10,000,000 or $20 per capita. The consumption of malt was about 2,200,000 bushels, and of hops 1,525, 000 pounds. The breweries of Cincinnati employ a vast number of men. Wages are good, from that of the brewmaster at from $15,000 a year to $7,500, down to the common laborer, who gets $1.50 a day and all the beer he can drink. This industry of the city is one of its most progressive and valuable. Its wage rolls are immense, and this money finds its way into the various channels of trade.[1]

This survey of Cincinnati's brewing industry clearly underscores its significance for the economic life of the region, and that Cincinnati was unquestionably one of the major brewing centers in the United States. However, problems loomed on the horizon. In the short term, there was also the loss of several members of the family, and in the long term, the unforeseen specter of World War I and Prohibition.

Wilhelm Moerlein (1865–96)

Although the brewing industry was burgeoning in the 1890s, the Moerlein family faced another unexpected loss in the family with the death of Christian Moerlein's son Wilhelm, who had served on the board of the company as secretary. Wilhelm was born 19 November 1865 and had attended public and private schools in Cincinnati, and graduated from Gambier College in Gambier, Ohio. Thereafter, he traveled across the country and Europe before taking a position in 1891 as treasurer of the Moerlein Brewing Company. On 21 May of the same year, he wed Carolina Baier, and they had one son, Christian, named in honor of his grandfather. Beginning in 1895, however, Wilhelm became afflicted with chest pains, and traveled to Europe in the hope of resting and getting his health back. Upon returning to Cincinnati, the Moerlein family brought him out West, but unfortunately to no avail. After returning home, he passed away 17 September 1896.[2]

Wilhelm Moerlein gravesite at Spring Grove Cemetery.

John Goetz, Jr. (1855–99)

John Goetz, Jr., played an important role in the 1890s not only as vice president of the company, but also as a widely respected member of the community. Although not as flamboyant as George Moerlein, Goetz was an accomplished vice president of the brewery. Although other members of the Moerlein family held memberships in various German-American societies, it was Goetz who actually played a leading role in German-American community affairs. According to *Cincinnati und sein Deutschthum*,

> As long as the sound of our dear German mother tongue area is heard in Cincinnati and so long as a German heart beats in Cincinnati, then so long will the name of John Goetz, Jr. endure in loving remembrance. The German element of Cincinnati has many a son, and many a proud name can be mentioned, but a better, more loyal son than John Goetz, Jr. cannot be found.

It noted that although many Cincinnatians mourned his demise, his loss was most deeply felt by German-Americans. Goetz's stature in the German-American community no doubt contributed to the popularity of Moerlein beer, especially among the many German societies and organizations. Goetz, it noted, was "wholeheartedly an American, a true son of our glorious and great Republic. He was, however, also just as good of a German. German in thought and speech, he honored and treasured German customs and traditions."[3]

John Goetz, Jr.

Born in Cincinnati on 28 January 1855, Goetz attended public schools in Cincinnati, and graduated in 1876 from the Cincinnati Law School, after which he began the practice of law. After serving as assistant city solicitor, Goetz took a position with the Moerlein Brewing Company, and rose to become a vice president alongside brother-in-law George. In 1888, he was appointed to the Board of Fire Commissioners by the mayor, and was reappointed continually, holding the office until his death, also serving as president of the board. Goetz also served as assistant city treasurer. Additionally, he served as president of the Lincoln Club and the Cincinnati Centennial Exposition of 1888.

In 1895, Heinrich A. Rattermann, the well-known historian and

John Goetz, Jr., gravesite at Spring Grove Cemetery.

editor of the historical journal *Der Deutsche Pionier*, organized a festival honoring 6 October, the date on which in 1683 the first German settlement had been established at Germantown, Pennsylvania.[4] This followed up on the celebration he had organized in 1883 for the bicentennial of the founding of Germantown. Thereafter, the question arose as to whether this should be held on an annual basis. After the 1895 celebration, Goetz helped organized the German Day Society, thus ensuring German Day would be held annually. Initially, he served on its board of directors and then was elected the society's president in 1898. Thanks in great part to Goetz, Cincinnati now has one of the oldest annual German Day celebrations in the United States.

Additionally Goetz was actively involved in organizing the fiftieth anniversary of the National Saengerfest of the Federation of German-American Singing Societies (*Nord-amerikanischer Saengerbund*) in 1899, serving on the organizational committee as vice president.[5]

In 1881, Goetz married Christian Moerlein's daughter Elizabeth (1860–1925), and they had two children, Christian and Emma. Their family residence in Clifton Heights is today's well-known Lenhardt's

Restaurant. Goetz's sudden and untimely death on 23 January 1899 deprived the brewing company not only of one of its important board members, but the German-American community of one of its most widely respected spokesmen. A special memorial service, sponsored by the German Day Society, was held in his honor at Spring Grove Cemetery on 10 September 1900 and attended by family, friends, and countless members and representatives of the German societies of the area.

John Moerlein (1846–1921)

After the death of Christian Moerlein in 1897, the leadership fell to his son John (1846–1921), who took over as president, remaining in that position until the company closed down operations. Moving up from the office of treasurer to serve as vice president was his younger and sole surviving brother Jacob (1855–1912). Their mother, Barbara Moerlein, née Oeh, passed away shortly after the turn of the century. Fortunately, another star was on the horizon in the family.

J. George Jung (1859–1927)

Stepping up to serve as secretary and treasurer of the brewery was J. George Jung (1859–1927). In the 1900s, he took on the job of serving as general manager and, after the death of John Moerlein, served as the last president of the company. Jung was an active member of various societies, belonging to several lodges, as well as the Cincinnati Club. Most importantly, he was a member of the Moerlein family. Jung's home was an impressive red-brick house on Whitfield Avenue in Clifton.

Jung's father, Philipp (1825–1916) was from the town of Haschbach in the Bavarian Palatinate and came to America with three of his brothers in 1847. His brother Daniel (1822–77) was the first member of the family to immigrate, coming to America in 1837. He first settled in Buffalo, New York, where he was apprenticed as a blacksmith.

J. George Jung
Cartoon from the local press.

He then moved to Akron, Ohio, where he opened his own business. In 1841, he moved to Cincinnati, but in 1846 returned to Haschbach for a visit, coming back to Cincinnati the next year with his three brothers. Daniel's brothers were also blacksmiths and may have apprenticed with Moerlein, as they stayed with him after arriving in Cincinnati.

In 1849 Moerlein married Barbara Oeh (1827–1903) and likely introduced her sister Magdalena Oeh (1830–1915) to Philipp, as they were married in 1852. The Oeh family came from Oberfellendorf in Upper Franconia, which is located not far from Moerlein's home town of Truppach. The two families thus got connected initially by means of the blacksmithing trade and then by marriage. Both families remained lifelong friends with the Jung family living on Ohio Avenue near the uptown home of Christian Moerlein. According to Ron Shepherd, a descendant of the Jung family, Philipp Jung became a wagonmaker and did quite well with his business "and very likely had one very good customer for his wagons—Moerlein Brewing."[6]

In 1854 Daniel Jung, who had been the first of the Jung brothers to immigrate, opened a brewery, together with Peter Weyand, at the site of his blacksmith shop on Central Avenue. This became known as the Western Brewery, later moving to larger facilities at the corner of Freeman and Bank Streets. After Weyand's death in 1875, the business became known as the Jung Brewing Company and lasted until 1919 when it closed as a result of Prohibition. Since Moerlein opened his brewery in 1853 on Elm Street where his blacksmith shop was located, it seems likely that Daniel Jung made the same decision the following year in switching from blacksmithing to brewing. Both saw that brewing beer was more profitable than shoeing horses.[7]

It made perfect sense to have J. George Jung on the management team of the brewery, since he was a nephew of Barbara and Christian Moerlein and their sons were Jung's cousins. This was in line with the Moerlein Brewing Company as a family run business. Additionally, Jung's cousins ran the Jung Brewing Company.

Sadly, it was Jung's task to close down the affairs of the company his uncle had founded. Had he lived as long as Christian Moerlein, he might have been the one with the knowledge and abilities who could have orchestrated a comeback for the brewery after the revocation of Prohibition, because he was the last member of the family to have occupied a key position in the brewery.[8]

George Moerlein (1859–1932)

In addition to the family members discussed above, there were other members of the Moerlein family that should be mentioned. George Moerlein was born in Bayreuth in 1859 and came to America in 1882, settling not surprisingly in Cincinnati. According to his obituary in the annual report of the German Pioneer Society, he was involved in the brewing industry, but later on, no doubt after the onset of Prohibition, was engaged in farming at his farm on Springfield Road in Colerain Township. The city directories (1900 and 1905) indicate that he was employed at the Christian Moerlein Brewery as a bookkeeper. He is buried at St. Mary Cemetery in Cincinnati.[9]

Andrew Moerlein (1864–1915)

Andrew Moerlein (1864–1915) was also born in Bayreuth and came to America in the fall of 1883. We know that he was not Christian's nephew, a son of his brother Johann Georg, as records at Spring Grove Cemetery, where he is buried, indicate that his parents were Peter and Catherine Moerlein. He therefore must have been the son of one of Christian Moerlein's cousins and likely was a brother of George Moerlein who arrived in Cincinnati a year before. Like George, Andrew Moerlein also found employment at the brewery, his position being that of stall boss, or stable boss. This was no doubt an important position given the Moerlein stable and the large number of horses maintained by the brewery for delivery purposes. From his obituary in an annual report of the German Pioneer Society, we know that Andrew Moerlein was, like George, also a member of that group.[10] His place of residence was in the Mohawk section of Over-the-Rhine, which was just around the corner from the Moerlein Brewery.

End of an Era

The brewery continued to the onset of Prohibition. Together with his extended family, Christian Moerlein had established one of the nation's leading breweries. Their brewery was the largest in the state of Ohio and one of the five largest in the United States. It had acquired a national and international reputation and the Moerlein family had emerged as one of the great brewing family dynasties in America.[11] Moreover, it had survived the loss of several key players in the family-run business.

New and unforeseen challenges were now on the horizon for the Christian Moerlein Brewing Company. It would now have to face Prohibition, this following hard on the heels of World War I with all the anti-German hysteria and sentiment that came along with it. The war and Prohibition spelled hard times for German-Americans in general and for the brewing industry in particular, both leaving lasting marks on the city of Cincinnati, especially the Over-the-Rhine district.

CHAPTER 10

The Dark Ages

World War I

IF THE PREWAR ERA WAS THE GOLDEN AGE for the German heritage in general and for the brewing industry in particular, then World War I marked the onset of the Dark Ages. It lasted a total of sixteen years—from American entrance into World War I in 1917 till the end of Prohibition in 1933.

The text of an Ohio Historical Society marker entitled "The Anti-German Hysteria," located at Findlay Market in the Over-the-Rhine district, briefly and succinctly describes the World War I era and its impact on the German heritage.

> The United States' declaration of war on Germany in April 1917 resulted in a tragic display of hysteria directed against everything and anything German. In Cincinnati, German teachers were dismissed from public schools, German professors were censored, German collections and publications were removed from circulation at the Public Library, businesses with German names had their names 'Americanized' and, by police order, only English language public meetings could be held.

Side two states,

> As a result of the anti-German hysteria during World War I, name changing became the rage. The Cincinnati City Council followed the trend by changing German street names on April 9, 1918. Among those changed were: German Street to English Street, Berlin Street to Woodrow Street, Bremen Street to Republic Street, Brunswick Street to Edgecliff Point, Frankfort Street to Connecticut Street, Hanover Street to Yukon Street, Hapsburg Street to Merrimac Street, Schumann Street to Meredith Street, Vienna Street to Panama Street, and Humboldt Street to Taft Road.

Cincinnati Post announces the end of World War I.

The First World War came to an end in November 1918 and was followed soon thereafter in January 1919, by the passage of the Eighteenth Amendment by Congress. Another war now began, this time against the brewing industry. Later that year (October 1919), the National Prohibition Act introduced by Rep. Andrew J. Volstead of Minnesota, was passed to enforce Prohibition. Seeing the handwriting on the wall, most breweries began to shut down operations. J. George Jung, secretary and treasurer of the Christian Moerlein Brewing Company, announced on 1 June 1919 that the brewery would follow suit.

Most of the property of the brewery was sold by 1921, although the Elm Street office was maintained until 1924. Thereafter, the remaining affairs of the company were moved to the Provident Bank Building with Jung serving now as the company's president.

Prohibition

The national disaster known as Prohibition came along right after World War I, bringing many fine breweries to an abrupt end, including the Christian Moerlein Brewing Company. After closing its plant, it would be more than half a century before beer bearing the legendary name of Christian Moerlein would again appear on a brew in the Queen City of the West. In spite of the demise of the company, its reputation lived on as a memorable part of the area's brewing heritage.

Prohibition was doomed from the beginning. So profoundly wrong was it that it is incomprehensible that it ever became law. German-Americans objected to it for two basic reasons: First, beer was considered a dietary ingredient, and even referred to it as *flüssiges Brot* (liquid bread). Historically, beer was not only part of the diet, but an essential part of social life, especially in the festivities sponsored by the many German-American societies. Second, their objections were based on deeply held philosophical views about the role of government and their belief in "personal liberty." They felt that government had no right to regulate what the individual should, or should not drink, and to do so was an infringement on the rights of the individual.

Prohibition would never have been enacted had it not ridden the crest of the wave of anti-German hysteria engendered by World War I. Beer and brewing were identified with the German element, as most brewers in the United States were of German descent, and the brew they favored, lager beer, had come to America as a result of German immigration. Moreover, German-American brewers were often not only members of German-American societies, but frequently served as their leaders. This clearly was the case in Cincinnati.

The German-American Alliance of Cincinnati served as the umbrella organization for the more than one hundred German societies of the area and grew out of the German Day Society founded in 1896. The alliance played an active role in local affairs. Two major planks in its platform were support for German bilingual instruction in the public schools and opposition to Prohibition. The Cincinnati Alliance was affiliated with the German-American Alliance of Ohio, a confederation of local branches of the Alliance, which in turn belonged to the National German-American Alliance. Judge John Schwaab served as president of the German-American Alliance of Cincinnati as well as the German-American Alliance of Ohio. Additionally, he held office as a vice president of the National German-American Alliance. The Cincinnati Alliance thus played a role not only in local affairs, but statewide as well, even exerting national influence by means of its president.

Are You a Loyal Citizen?

If You Are, You Cannot Vote to Maintain the Disloyal, Pro-German Beer Interests of Ohio

The United States is at war with Germany.

Uncle Sam says, "*I want your boy to fight in the trenches.*" You may not want to give your boy, but you bow to the will of the government, and your boy leaves home for the uncertainties of war.

Uncle Sam says to you, "*I want your money to help pay the expenses of this war,*" and he takes your money and your property to help make this country and the world safe for democracy. As patriotic citizens, you give your boy and your money to the public good.

Save! Save! Save!

Uncle Sam says we must conserve our grain and foodstuffs in this world crisis. We must feed our armies and furnish food for the hungry and starving of the other countries. "Aye!" "Aye!" is the general response.

The housewives are urged to save a slice of bread a day. "Save!" Save!" is the cry which is going up all over the land.

But the pro-German beer interests say, "*We will not save. We will go on wasting 3,390,000,000 pounds of foodstuff a year in the making of beer, and if you dare attempt to stop us, we will throttle legislation and not permit Congress to enact necessary war measures.*'

Now the same pro-German brewers are pleading with Ohio citizens to vote November 6 to approve their disloyalty and permit them to continue the waste of foodstuffs in the making of beer.

Tens of thousands of Germans here in Ohio, and elsewhere, are as much opposed to the plans of these pro-German brewers and as heartily in favor of the overthrow of beer autocracy as any class of people in this country. These Germans are good citizens, loyal Amer-

Anti-German poster encouraging support of Prohibition.

The German-American Alliance of Cincinnati had a strong record of opposition to Prohibition. On 1 August 1914 it had opened its campaign against Prohibition with a mass meeting, and its president, Judge John Schwaab, declared that "Prohibition is a fight against the Germans." And that year, the German-American Alliance of Ohio collected a petition with 280,000 signatures against Prohibition. In July 1915, Schwaab claimed that "The drink question is forced upon us by the same hypocritical Puritans as over there are endeavoring to exterminate the German nation."[1]

In 1919, the U.S. Senate issued a report, whose title alone spoke volumes: *Brewing and Liquor Interests and German and Bolshevik Propaganda*. It referred to the so-called "liquor traffic" as "a vicious interest" that had been unpatriotic because it had been "pro-German in its sympathies and conduct."[2] It also asserted that the National German-American Alliance had been mainly funded and sponsored by brewers across America. Prohibition was, therefore, clearly linked to the anti-German sentiment of the time. And, not surprisingly so, since the major breweries were owned and operated by German-Americans. Indeed, trying to find a non-German name in the brewing industry was if not rare, well nigh impossible.

Impact of Prohibition

When the Volstead Act went into effect in 1919, the German-American Alliance of Cincinnati held final fest as a huge "wake" mourning the demise of beer. In my book on the Cincinnati Germans after World War I, I described the impact of Prohibition on the German-American community as follows:

From *Cincinnati Germans After the Great War*
by Don Heinrich Tolzmann

Prohibition deprived German social life of an essential element. The Bavarian Singers explained, "Our losses were mainly due to the unmentionable Prohibition, bringing with it a decline of visitors to our celebrations and a corresponding loss in revenue and surpluses." Carl Pletz, former editor of the now defunct *Volksblatt*, lamented that "there was no longer a good draft beer to be had, and the main attraction for a congenial get-together no longer exists." Also the Stammtisch "had almost completely disappeared from many an inn." Most societies would agree with the observations of the Pionier-Verein that dry society meetings were "unthinkable" and the near-beer was a mediocre substitute for the real beer. Under Prohibition "the minutes are read, the secretary replying monotonously: absent. After a good half hour it is time to go home. Such is the course of business," according to the secretary of one society.

Throughout the 1920s German-Americans of Cincinnati voiced opposition to Prohibition. Charles Schmidt, president of the North American Saengerbund and the Vereinigte Saenger of Cincinnati, spoke 12 July 1921 at the 53rd Foundation Festival of the Pionier-Verein, and expressed the hope that the new president, Harding, would see the evil of Prohibition. According to him, beer, wine, and schnapps had earlier brought in tax money for the government, but now nothing. Now one had to be sick in order to get something to drink. However, beer was more than a tonic, according to Schmidt, it was "Teutonic." Moreover, all the products used for brewing were American grown, and those who brewed and drank it were "good Americans."

At the 49th Foundation Festival of the German Literary Club in 1926 Prohibition provided the basis for satire in song:

> Wir sind für feuchte Planke,
> Verflucht sei der Gedanke,
> Entalkoholisiert!

> ———

> We are for "wet" party planks,
> Cursed be the thought
> Of Prohibition!

The societies had no choice but to accept Prohibition, while longing for its conclusion. The main speaker, Alfred K. Nippert, at the Washington Fest of the Pionier-Verein, 23 February 1928, described Prohibition as a threat to personal liberty. At another Foundation Festival of the Verein, in 1928, Erich Becker referred to the reform movement as the basic flaw in America. This reform movement had led to the evil known as Prohibition, according to him. He noted that just as the repulsive war was over the German-Americans had blessed with Prohibition.

Prohibition was difficult to enforce in Cincinnati. In 1929, 490 bootleggers were arrested and the town was honeycombed with home brew parlors, speakeasies, and private clubs. Some of the brewing companies were forced out of business. The Moerlein Co. closed its plant in 1919 and the Hauck Brewing Company followed suit in March 1927. By 1933 all breweries had ceased production of beer except Bruckmann's, which produced near beer. In March 1933 the production of light wine and 3.2 beer was allowed, and Ohio revoked the Prohibition Act and the city council passed an emergency ordinance legalizing the production of beer. In April 1933 beer was again legal in Cincinnati. Bruckmann's swiftly ran out of all its beer so that some had to be imported from Louisville, Chicago, and Colorado. Some brewers decided to start again after 13 years of Prohibition, but only three pre-Prohibition brewers survived: Hudepohl, Foss-Schneider, and Schaller Brothers. By 1935, a total of 1,114,000 barrels of beer were being produced.

H. L. Mencken wrote, "Prohibition went into effect on January 15, 1920 and blew up at last on December 5, 1933—an elapsed time of twelve years, ten months and nineteen days. It seemed almost a geologic epoch while it was going on, and the human suffering that it entailed must have been a fair match for that of the Black Death of the Thirty Years War . . . "

The years left their mark on Cincinnati. Gone were the family beer gardens, sitting rooms, and nickel beer which had brought people together in the community. No longer would they serve as centers of social, civic, and business life. They were replaced by a new institution, the dimly lit tavern. Grammer's and Mecklenburg's were among the few remaining restaurants and beer gardens. Over-the-Rhine had lost an elemental flavor and atmosphere with the loss of many restaurants, concert halls, and beer gardens. No longer would there be family Sunday afternoons in the beer garden accompanied by the little bands playing strains of Strauss and oom-pah music.[3]

Aftermath

Prohibition struck a blow at social life in the Greater Cincinnati area, especially in the Over-the-Rhine district, where so many breweries, beer gardens, saloons, concert halls, restaurants, and cafes had been located. Moreover, the economic impact was devastating when one considers all the people employed in these and related businesses and industries. As noted earlier, German-Americans particularly objected to laws banning what historically was considered a "dietary ingredient," as well as a basic element of German social life. Most importantly, Prohibition was considered an infringement on "personal liberty" and contrary to the belief that government had no right to legislate what an individual should, or should not drink.

Prohibition also greatly affected brewing families. They and their breweries stood in a symbiotic relationship with each other: breweries depended on families to run them, but families were also held together by the very nature of their companies. The same can be said for other kinds of family run businesses. Once breweries closed down, very few of them reopened after Prohibition and the families that ran them had to move on with their lives, some continuing to play an active role in the community in other fields of endeavor, such as the Hauck family, while others did not.[4] This was the case with the Moerlein family, whose direct descendants no longer live in the area, making for the virtual disappearance of the family in the hometown of the Moerlein Brewery.

CHAPTER 11

The Moerlein Legacy

After Prohibition

WAS AN ATTEMPT MADE TO REOPEN THE MOERLEIN BREWERY after
Prohibition? In his history of the brewing industry in Cincinnati,
Timothy J. Holian tells us what happened then.

> Despite early proclamations from Moerlein management that
> the company had no intention to return to brewing activity,
> President Joseph H. Assel, announced on September 15, 1933,
> that a new brewery was to be constructed on a thirty acre
> tract of land at Paddock Road and Tennessee Avenue, along
> the Baltimore and Ohio Road line and with a further connec-
> tion to the Norfolk and Western system. Further details held
> that construction of the new facility would start around Octo-
> ber 1, and beginning early in 1934 the business would com-
> mence an annual output of some 500,000 barrels produced by
> 500 employees. Yet ultimately nothing materialized out of the
> plan, nor did the company attempt to revitalize its former
> brewery holdings on Elm Street.[1]

How can we explain the company's failure to stage a comeback? It
was no doubt due to the costs involved and it should be recalled that

this was the time of the Great Depression and risking the expense of starting anew, even if success in brewing might look like a sure thing, would still have been a costly venture. However, this is probably only part of the answer.

A key factor goes back to the very nature of the company as a family enterprise. In 1921, the last pre-Prohibition president of the brewery, John Moerlein, passed away, preceded in death by his younger brother, Jacob (1912), as well as Jacob's son, George (1917). And then the last president of the company, J. George Jung passed away (1927). Two additional losses in the 1930s were Christian's great-grandson Jacob, the son of his grandson George, who died in 1931 at the age of twenty-eight and William, the son of Wilhelm, who died in 1935 at the age of forty-two.

By 1935, six members of the family had passed away in a little more than twenty years. When the family suffered several deaths in the 1890s, it was able to overcome the loss as there was still a reservoir of family members to draw from, but this apparently was not the case by the 1930s.

Joseph H. Assel, who married the widow of George Moerlein, undertook some initial plans, but ones that ultimately did not come to fruition due to the aforementioned reasons. However, the fact, that he was part of the Moerlein clan illuminates the family nature of the business, and its attempt at addressing the question of staging a comeback.

Businesses come and go depending on a plethora of factors, but those that are family based can last for generations, with the key element being the existence of a viable family network with a sufficient number of members who can fill the ranks of the management team. This is what the Moerlein Brewing Company had been before Prohibition, but now lacked the necessary forces to bring about a comeback.

Legacy

A company as large and influential as the Christian Moerlein Brewing

Company was bound to have a legacy. The dictionary definition of legacy is that which is "handed down from an ancestor or a predecessor or from the past." There are numerous dimensions of the legacy of the Christian Moerlein Brewing Company. Some of these relate to the historical memory of the company and legendary reputation it enjoys in the region.

Additionally, there are the more tangible aspects, such as artifacts, objects, and other memorabilia produced by the brewery. These items are highly valued and sought after as collectibles today.[2] An additional part of the Moerlein legacy is the Charles Moerlein Foundation located with the Fifth Third Bank of Cincinnati. Established by Charles Moerlein (1878–1966), this charitable foundation was created in the 1940s by the son of John Moerlein, who served as brewery's last president before Prohibition.

More durable, however, probably in the long run, is the example set by Christian Moerlein and which defined the legacy for which he is known. Basically, this consists of two images we have of him: the self-made man and the beer baron.

At the very center of the Moerlein legacy stands the person of Christian Moerlein, the self-made man, who founded and built the company, thereby realizing the American Dream. The ideal of the American Dream relates to the "Horatio Alger myth," which arose in the nineteenth century. So-called because it developed out of the novels written by Horatio Alger, Jr., this myth revolved around individuals who were able to rise from "rags to riches."[3] J. H. Strasser, a German-American journalist, qualified the Horatio Alger myth by explaining the requirements: "By means of hard work and thriftiness, you can make it here . . . and attain a relative degree of success."[4]

Note that Strasser does not say that anyone can rise from rags to riches, but rather offers the more realistic advice that one could "attain a relative degree of success" by means of "hard work and thriftiness." This notion was widely expressed in various forms by German-American authors and journalists, and might best be described as the German-American vision and version of the Horatio Alger myth, and one that was not a myth, but rather a pathway open to all who would apply themselves accordingly. Certainly, Christian Moerlein provides a model in this regard by having lived a life that gave credence to the realities of the American Dream, as well as the Horatio Alger myth.

In addition to the legacy of the self-made man, there also exists today the popular image of Christian Moerlein as the gregarious and flamboyant beer baron. At the heart of this popular image are the character traits that defined his public persona, but which in time also came to incorporate elements drawn from his more flamboyant son George Moerlein and German community leader and son-in-law John Goetz, Jr. The popular beer baron image we have today of Christian Moerlein might best be viewed as a composite image of the three of them. They come together to embellish and enhance the legendary image of Christian Moerlein. This in itself is a powerful and enduring legacy. Man and myth merge in Christian Moerlein to become a legend.

The image of Moerlein as a self-made man and beer baron come together to present the *Gesamtbild* (general image) of him. He is the ambitious, hardworking, diligent businessman who built a brewing empire based on family, even as he projected a skillfully crafted and finely polished image that captivated the public at large. This image was not only effective at the time it emerged, but proved to be enduring in the creation of a reputation that developed into legendary proportions.

CHAPTER 12

The Moerlein Renaissance

Return of Moerlein Beer

RENEWED INTEREST IN MOERLEIN BREWS began in 1981 when the Hudepohl Brewing Company brought the Moerlein name back again with its highly successful Christian Moerlein Select Lager. According to Greg Hardman,

> That beer was arguably the best craft beer east of the Mississippi. It was almost five years before Sam Adams launched in the U.S., and the gentleman who devised it was Bob Pohl from the Hudepohl Brewing Company. After he brewed this great Munich Helles Lager, he did something so ingenious. He got it named the first American beer to pass the German Purity Laws and I have the letter to this today from the German government.[1]

Moerlein Select Lager was followed soon thereafter by its Christian Moerlein Doppel Dark Beer. In 1986, Hudepohl was acquired by Schoenling to form the Hudepohl-Schoenling Brewing Company, which unfortunately closed down in 1999.[2] Nevertheless, it had contributed greatly to bringing the Moerlein name back as a product that signified quality beer in the Greater Cincinnati area and beyond.

The New Christian Moerlein Brewing Company

In 2004 Greg Hardman succeeded in bringing the Christian Moerlein Brewing Company back to life. As president and CEO, he assembled all the previous brands owned by the Hudepohl-Schoenling Brewing Company, including Little Kings Cream Ale, Hudepohl, Hudy Delight, and Burger, and within several years had succeeded in making the new Christian Moerlein Brewing Company one of the leading craft breweries in the country.

Prior to taking on the task of recreating the Christian Moerlein Brewing Company, Hardman had spent eighteen years with Warsteiner Importers Agency, a subsidiary of Warsteiner Brauerei KG, Warstein, Germany, a leading brewer of beer throughout the world. From 1997 to 2004, Hardman had served as president and CEO of Warsteiner Importers Agency's North American operation.[3]

According to Hardman, "I just felt that it was my mission to bring these brands back to their rightful position and by doing that and putting a good quality product in front of people and showing them you

Greg Hardman at the construction site of the new Moerlein Lager House
with the Roebling Suspension Bridge in the background.
Fall 2011

had a little passion behind it, people would actually gravitate to those brands." He also notes that "I just felt as though there's always a loyalty for a beloved local brand, that Cincinnati would come along for the ride and they are." He also explains that "I am not doing anything spectacular, just what should have been done all along with Cincinnati's beer brands. I look at it as evolving the brands, not preserving them. I'm not bringing you your daddy's Moerlein. I'm going to bring you what Moerlein should have been. It was a world-class beer."[4]

In April 2010, the Christian Moerlein Brewing Company issued the following press release:

MOERLEIN, HUDEPOHL, SCHOENLING, BURGER AND LITTLE KINGS ALL COMING HOME

CHRISTIAN MOERLEIN BREWING COMPANY ANNOUNCES PLANS TO OPEN BREWING OPERATIONS IN CINCINNATI'S HISTORIC OVER-THE-RHINE BREWERY DISTRICT

FIRST MOERLEIN TO BE BREWED IN OVER-THE-RHINE SINCE START OF PROHIBITION IN 1919

CINCINNATI, OHIO — April 16, 2010 — Christian Moerlein Brewing Company and its wholly owned subsidiary Hudepohl-Schoenling Brewing Co. is announcing plans to expand brewing operations to Cincinnati's historic Over-the-Rhine Brewery District. The site of the new brewing operation will be the former Husman Potato Chip plant located 1621 Moore Street just north of Liberty and east of Vine. "We are proud to be part of the continued renaissance and economic development of Over-the-Rhine," said Greg Hardman, president and CEO of Christian Moerlein Brewing Company.

> Our goal is to strategically implement a phased in production over the next two years from both existing production on some of our specialty beers and from the continued rapid growth of our brands," said Greg Hardman. The company has entered into a lease agreement with an option to buy for the 125,000 square foot facility that will enable the company to expand their business for many years to come; additionally, the buildings' sound infrastructure and historical significance were main considerations in choosing the Over-the-Rhine location. The site was also the malt and lager house of the former Kaufman Brewing Company from 1869 through 1919 (till start of Prohibition). . . . The history of Christian Moerlein dates back 157 years to when the brew master Christian Moerlein, an immigrant from Truppach, Bavaria, Germany brewed his first beer in Cincinnati's Over-the-Rhine Brewery District in 1853. Christian Moerlein ceased operations at the start of

Prohibition and did not resume operations after Prohibition ended in 1933. In 1981, Christian Moerlein was brought back to the Cincinnati market by the Hudepohl Brewing Company as one of the first commercially sold American craft beers and the first American beer to certifiably pass the German Purity Law of 1516 known as the Reinheitsgebot. Local ownership of the brand was lost when out of town owners purchased the brand assets of the Hudepohl-Schoenling Brewing Company in 1999 and later moved production to Maryland. Beer industry veteran and greater Cincinnati resident Greg Hardman purchased Christian Moerlein in 2004 bringing back the local ownership along with an additional commitment to bring back the local brewing heritage . . .

Christian Moerlein Brewing Company is the brewer of hand-crafted Moerlein Lagers & Ales including Moerlein O.T.R. Ale, Moerlein Lager House, Moerlein Barbarossa Double Dark Lager, Moerlein Northern Liberties IPA, Moerlein Fifth & Vine Oktoberfest Marzen, Moerlein Christkindl Winter Warmer Ale, Moerlein Friend of an Irishman Stout and Moerlein Emancipator Doppelbock. . . . Hudepohl-Schoenling Brewing Co. is the brewer of Hudy Delight, Hudy 14-K, Burger Classic and Little Kings Cream Ale and is a wholly owned subsidiary of Christian Moerlein Brewing Co.

Moerlein beer coaster.

In addition to its facility in Over-the-Rhine, the new Moerlein Brewing Company also opened its Moerlein Lager House on the Cincinnati riverfront on Monday, 27 February 2012, thus solidifying its foundations, as well as those of Cincinnati's renewed and revitalized brewing heritage. Located alongside the Great American Ball Park, the new Lager House provides panoramic views of the Ohio River, Covington and Newport, Kentucky, as well as the Roebling Suspension Bridge. In honor of Cincinnati's brewing heritage it features the Beer Baron's Hall of Fame and the grand staircase mural of Cincinnati's beer barons by artist Jim Effler.

Cincinnati's German Brewing Heritage

Several factors have contributed to bringing about the brewing renaissance of recent years, but Cincinnati's German heritage no doubt has played a major role. Where Germans settle, breweries soon emerge, as beer is considered a dietary ingredient and an integral part of social life. The brewing of lager beer in Cincinnati followed soon after the arrival of the first waves of German immigration to the area, with most of the breweries being located in the Over-the-Rhine district and the nearby West End. In the nineteenth century, Cincinnati became well known along with Milwaukee and Saint Louis as one of the three cities that formed the famed "German Triangle," a term coined for the three major German heritage centers in the United States.

Cincinnati remains to this day a city known for its many German festivals sponsored by area German societies. They are affiliated with the German-American Citizens League (GACL), the umbrella organization of thirty societies, which sponsor a wide array of festivals throughout the year, ranging from Maifest to Schuetzenfest and Oktoberfest, all of them featuring a wide variety of American and German beers. Such events have provided fertile ground for the brewing industry and for the emergence of craft brewing in the area.

The close connection between the brewing industry and the German-American community is underscored by the fact that John Goetz, Jr., vice president of the Moerlein Brewing Company, served in the 1890s as president of the German Day Society, the forerunner of today's GACL. Since 1895 it has not only sponsored the annual German Day, but has also supported other German-style festivals.

In 1972, the GACL suggested that a citywide Oktoberfest be held in downtown Cincinnati. Its president then, Helmut Maurer, commented that an Oktoberfest could be "based on the city's brewing heritage. We have some of the greatest breweries in the world here. And beer cuts across all backgrounds. Beer is Oktoberfest." Maurer noted the importance of heritage, saying that "Those of us with German-American origins feel this particularly. We see our children growing up in a society which does not clarify values for the young. We do not want this void to be part of their heritage and so we try to fill the gaps."[5]

The GACL went on to win the support of the Chamber of Commerce for a citywide Oktoberfest as a way of celebrating German heritage during the American Bicentennial in 1976. It also successfully enlisted the support of the local breweries, which enthusiastically joined the event as cosponsors. Since that time, Oktoberfest Zinzinnati has gone on to become an annual event, as well as the largest such festival held outside of Cincinnati's sister city of Munich. The fest now features American and German beers, as well as, of course, Christian Moerlein beers.

In 1992, the first annual Bockfest took place in the Over-the-Rhine district, an event which now has grown to become one of the largest festivals in Cincinnati. The event now begins at Arnold's Bar and Grill on Eighth Street and parades up Main Street. Since 2010, the parade has ended at the site of the new Christian Moerlein Brewery, which becomes Bockfest Hall for the entire first weekend in March. The ever-growing popularity of this festival showed the community-wide support and interest in the brewing heritage. Adding to the event's authenticity has been the cosponsorship of Bockfest by the GACL, which was one of the cofounders of the event.

Together with the Moerlein Brewing Company, the GACL held a series of keg tapping of Moerlein brews at several of the societies throughout the region, adding to their popularity. Moerlein is now available on tap at the clubhouses of the various German societies and featured at their festivals as well. This and other community events show how German heritage and beer go hand in hand.

Moerlein poster for keg tapping at the
Cincinnati Central Turners.

Additional interest in the German brewing heritage was reflected by the establishment of the Over-the-Rhine Brewery District in 2003. This historic district was formed by residents and business owners, who "recognized the unique history of this often ignored portion of Over-the-Rhine."[6] Of course the various buildings that once comprised the original Moerlein Brewing Company make up a foundational part of the historical district and are the focal point of tours throughout the area.

Bockfest parade—2010.

Muhlhauser Barn in West Chester, Ohio.

In 2008, the Muhlhauser Barn and Moerlein Gazebo were officially dedicated in Beckett Park in West Chester, located a few miles north of Cincinnati. Here several Cincinnati German beer barons had farms, where the necessary grain products for beer brewing were raised. The timber-frame barn built in 1881 for the Gottlieb Muhlhauser farm was thoroughly refurbished to become the centerpiece of the park, and although the Moerlein farm buildings had been torn down, the quaint Moerlein Gazebo with its fine copper roof was preserved and placed alongside the Muhlhauser Barn.[7]

Muhlhauser street sign in West Chester, Ohio.

On Saturday, 21 January 2012, a panel discussion was held at the downtown Public Library of Cincinnati on the topic of the Christian Moerlein Brewing Company. Panel participants included Gregory Hardman, CEO of the Moerlein Brewing Company; Steven Hampton, executive director of the Over-the-Rhine Brewing District; Michael Morgan, author and board member of the Over-the-Rhine Brewing District; and the author. Several hundred people gathered to hear the panel discuss the history of the original brewing company, as well as its more recent inception.

This and other recent developments testify to the ongoing interest in Cincinnati's German brewing heritage in general and Moerlein Brewing Company in particular and that Cincinnati has provided the right climate and fertile ground for their renaissance. This did not happen in a vacuum—Cincinnati was where it happened, a place that gave rise to a legendary beer baron: Christian Moerlein.[8]

CHAPTER 13

Moerlein Heritage Tour

Heritage Sites

FOR THOSE INTERESTED IN EXPLORING HISTORIC SITES, there are several worthy of visiting that relate directly or indirectly to the Moerlein Brewing Company. Taken together, they provide the basis for an interesting Moerlein Heritage Tour. The sites tell us much about Over-the-Rhine beer baron Christian Moerlein, his family, and his brewery.

Over-the-Rhine Sites

The Christian Moerlein Brewing Company was headquartered on Elm Street in the northwest section of the Over-the-Rhine district, just north of Findlay Market. The Moerlein brew house, which was located on the northeast corner of Elm and Henry Streets, was unfortunately torn down in 1947. It was a beautiful example of German-American brewing architecture built in the style known as *Rundbogenstil* (Romanesque Revival style).[1] This architectural style was used predominantly for secular buildings, such as breweries, and contrasted with Gothic, which was used mainly for churches in the Over-the-

Rhine district. These different styles send an immediate message that one style is mainly for secular, the other for religious structures. Altogether, a total of six buildings that were originally part of the Moerlein brewery are still extant today and convey an idea of the huge amount of space the company occupied, and consist of the following:

1. Christian Moerlein Barrel House
Location: 1910 Elm Street

The barrel house reminds us of the many related industries connected to the brewing industry, and which provided jobs to many in the area. Note the Rundbogenstil of this building. This building suffered a four-alarm fire in January 2010, but fortunately, the well-built structure survived relatively intact.

Christian Moerlein Barrel House.

2. Christian Moerlein Brewing Company Bottling Plant
Location: 1916 Elm Street

The bottling plant (1895), like the barrel house plant, reflected another industry related to the brewing industry that supplied many jobs to the region. It was built in the Renaissance Revival architectural style.

Christian Moerlein Brewing Company Bottling Plant.

3. Christian Moerlein Brewing Company Warehouse
Location: Corner of Dunlap and Henry Streets

As the largest brewery in the state of Ohio and one of the largest in the United States, the Moerlein Brewing Company no doubt had need to keep a significant stock on hand for shipping throughout the country, and this warehouse gives an indication of the size of stock it dealt with.

4. Christian Moerlein Brewing Company Icehouse
Location: Henry Street between Elm and Race Streets

This building, built in 1876, was housed to keep the beer cold and has a basement four stories deep. It now houses Apex Furniture. Machines for refrigeration were introduced in the 1870s, and became an important part of the brewing industry as they could produce ice throughout the year. Some local breweries built on the hillside north of the Moerlein brewery, so they could make use of tunnels, *Felsenkeller* (rock-lined cellars), built into the hillside, where beer could be kept cool.

Moerlein Icehouse.

5. Christian Moerlein Family Home
Location: 2017 Elm Street

Built in 1864, the family of Christian Moerlein resided here until 1870, when the family moved to its new home at 168 West Mulberry Street (now 18 Mulberry Street). They lived at the new address until 1882 when they moved to Clifton Heights. A tunnel from the basement of the house on Elm Street went under Elm Street, connecting the home to the building across the street.

Christian Moerlein Family Home at 2017 Elm Street.

6. Christian Moerlein Brewing Company Office Building
Location: 2019 Elm Street

The Moerlein office buildings date from 1878. Built in the Neo-Classical architectural style with a stone façade, it served as headquarters for the company down to the time of Prohibition. Note how Christian Moerlein conveniently built his office directly alongside his home, which had an underground tunnel connecting it with his brew house across the street. Moerlein thought out and planned well his brewery building, and this is clearly reflected in the way the buildings of his company are closely arranged and organized in this northwest corner of the Over-the-Rhine district.

Christian Moerlein Brewing Company office building.

7. Christian Moerlein Brewing Company Malt House
Location: 2025 Elm Street

The malt house is another indication of how many of the buildings of the Moerlein Brewing Company are still relatively intact in the Over-the-Rhine district.

Christian Moerlein Malt House (building on the right).

8. Bellevue Incline
Location: Intersection of Elm Street and McMicken Avenue

From this point, the Bellevue Incline, which was also called the Elm Street or Clifton Incline, carried passengers, vehicles, and streetcars up the hill to Ohio Avenue. The incline was constructed by the Cincinnati & Clifton Incline Railway, and was in operation from 1876 to 1926. This no doubt contributed to a greater amount of traffic between Over-the-Rhine and the Clifton Heights area atop the hill.

The creation of the incline reflects the growing population in Over-the-Rhine in the late nineteenth century. German-Americans began moving uphill to that area, including the Christian Moerlein family. The incline allowed for Moerlein and son-in-law Goetz, who also lived uptown, to easily commute back and forth from their hilltop homes to the brewery below in Over-the-Rhine.

The Bellevue Incline brought people to the Bellevue House, a beer garden and restaurant. Not surprisingly, the Bellevue House featured the fine brew of the Christian Moerlein Brewing Company. The Bellevue House was located at the top of the hill.

9. Brewery District Historical Marker
Location: 231 West McMicken Avenue

In 2008, this Ohio Historical Society marker was dedicated in honor of the many breweries in and around the Over-the-Rhine district. The text reads as follows:

> The Brewery District contains the majority of Cincinnati's remaining breweries and associated structures such as ice-

houses, bottling buildings, offices, and stables. With the first brewery north of Liberty Street founded in 1829, German immigrants fueled the growth of the brewing industry; by 1891, Cincinnati breweries produced over four barrels of beer per resident annually, almost twice as much as any other city in the nation. The brick breweries were typically designed in the Romanesque Revival style, and larger complexes often covered multiple city blocks. To produce the lager style beer common by 1860, typically very deep basements were dug or tunnels were cut into hillsides for the lagering process. At the height of production, eighteen of the twenty-six breweries in Greater Cincinnati were operating in Over-the-Rhine and the West End. Prohibition in 1919 closed most of the breweries permanently.

Brewery District Historical Marker.

10. Philippus Kirche—Philippus United Church of Christ
Location: 106 McMicken Avenue

The Moerleins were members of the Philippus Church, which was conveniently located down the hill from their uptown home on Ohio Avenue. The church was founded in 1890, and this building was built the year thereafter. Built in the Greek Revival style, Philippus presents a quite striking and impressive appearance with its red brick façade. German services were held regularly until the 1980s, and a German Christmas service continues to take place every year on Christmas Eve. Among the especially noteworthy features of this church are the following:

A. Finger Pointing to Heaven
Location: Atop the steeple on the Philippus Church

Known as the "Finger to Heaven," and also as the "Finger to God," the golden hand pointing heavenwards on the top of the church steeple of the Philippus United Church of Christ is one of the most striking landmarks in the area, especially from the hillsides overlooking the Over-the-Rhine district. Atop the steeple is a clenched golden hand with the index finger pointing to the heavens. It was placed there at the direction of the Rev. Dr. Jacob Pistor (1843–1914), founding pastor of the church. The church was designed by Anthony Kunz, who later established the firm of Anthony Kunz & Sons, Architects.

B. World War Memorial
Location: Front of the Philippus Church

In 1968, the church created a war memorial in honor of church members who served in the armed forces during the world wars by placing a U.S. soldier's helmet atop the cross above the entrance to the church.

C. Moerlein Organ
Location: Inside the Philippus Church

The interior of the church is beautifully surrounded by stained glass windows, and in the altar area is an organ dedicated to Christian Moerlein and his daughter Emma. The Moerlein family name can also be found on plaques inside the church as well.

Philippus Church and its World War memorial.

Plaque located in the Philippus Church and
dedicated to Christian Moerlein and his daughter Emma.

D. Stained Glass Windows
Location: Inside the Philippus Church

Inside the church there are a number of exceptionally beautiful stained glass windows with German inscriptions. For example, one noteworthy window is dedicated to the German-American brewer Gottlieb Mühlhäuser, (1836–1905), president and general manager of the Windisch-Muhlhauser Brewing Company. This particular window bears the inscription: *"Zum Andenken an Gottlieb Muhlhauser, Gewidmet von seiner Frau Christine B. Muhlhauser und Sohn Edward Muhlhauser"* (In Memory of Gottlieb Muhlhauser, dedicated by his wife Christine B. Muhlhauser and son Edward Muhlhauser)."

11. New Christian Moerlein Brewery
Location: 1621 Moore Street

This building is the site for the new Christian Moerlein Brewery founded by Greg Hardman. Previously it belonged to Husman Potato Chips and prior to that was part of the Kauffman Brewing Company that was headquartered on Vine Street. Since 2010, the building has also served as Bockfest Hall for the annual celebration of Bockfest.

Stained glass window inside the Philippus Church.

Clifton Heights

12. Christian Moerlein Family Home on Mulberry Street
Location: 18 Mulberry Street

The Christian Moerlein Family moved here in 1870 from their home on Elm Street and lived here until 1882 when the family moved to a home at 2407 Ohio Avenue. The Mulberry Street home is located one block east of Vine Street on Mulberry (see below).

13. Christian Moerlein Family Uptown Home
Location: 2407 Ohio Avenue

In 1882 the Moerlein family moved to this home from their previous home on Mulberry Street. Servant quarters were located behind this impressive three-story brick structure. The funeral service of Christian Moerlein was held here in 1897, with interment at Spring Grove Cemetery.

Front entrance to Christian Moerlein home at 18 Mulberry Street.

Christian Moerlein family uptown home at 2407 Ohio Avenue.

14. Bellevue Park
Location: Ohio Avenue and Parker Street

This park provides an excellent view of the Over-the-Rhine district, the Moerlein brewery building complex, and the downtown area of Cincinnati. After the Bellevue Incline closed in 1927, some of the land was acquired by the Cincinnati Park Board for the creation of Bellevue Park, which opened in 1936. This park is located where the Bellevue Incline arrived after departing from Elm Street in the Over-the-Rhine district below, bringing passengers, vehicles, and streetcars to this point. After the incline opened in 1876, the Bellevue House with an attached beer garden was opened here, specializing, not surprisingly, in the brews of the Christian Moerlein Brewing Company. It no doubt offered a convenient location for social get-togethers for members and friends of the Moerlein family. See illustration no. 8.

15. Moerlein Avenue Sign
Location: On West McMillan Street between the Moerlein and Goetz homes

This street honors Christian Moerlein and its location in Clifton Heights is due to Moerlein's uptown home.

16. John Goetz, Jr., Home
Location: 151 West McMillan Street

This was the home of Moerlein's son-in-law, John Goetz, Jr., (1855–99) and his daughter Elizabeth, and was given to the couple as a wedding present (1881) by Christian Moerlein and his wife, Barbara. In the 1960s, Anton and Emmy Lenhardt turned the home into Lenhardt's Restaurant, a well-known and popular German-Hungarian restaurant in Clifton Heights. An excellent item on the menu there consists of homemade sausage, sauerkraut, and potatoes, but there are many other fine offerings as well. Note the beautiful painting on the ceiling of the dining room, as well as the fine woodwork in the building.

17. J. George Jung Home
Location: 3430 Whitfield Avenue

The home of Christian Moerlein's nephew and the last president of the brewery.

Former home of John Goetz, Jr. Currently Lenhardt's Restaurant.

Former home of J. George Jung at 3430 Whitfield Avenue.

West Chester

---

18. Moerlein Gazebo
Location: Muhlhauser Barn and Moerlein Gazebo
Beckett Park, West Chester

The gazebo belonging to the Moerlein family is now located at the newly refurbished Muhlhauser Barn in West Chester. A brochure for the Muhlhauser Barn and Moerlein Gazebo in Beckett Park in West Chester states,

> The Muhlhauser and Moerlein names are among the most recognizable in Butler County. Their families maintained summer homes here and operated some of the largest farms in the area catering to the production of beer. In 1866, Gottlieb Muhlhauser joined forces with Conrad Windisch and started the Windisch-Muhlhauser Brewing Co. The 1881 timber-frame barn once used in the Muhlhauser farming operation is one of the few of its kind remaining in Ohio. The barn is now the centerpiece of West Chester's Beckett Park in Union Centre and is available for parties, reunions, meetings and other gatherings. The Moerlein Gazebo, also at Beckett Park, once graced the lawn of the stately Moerlein family home on Port Union Road near the West Chester Township boundary. . . . The home was torn down in the 1990s, but the charming copper-roofed gazebo was donated to West Chester Township.

The Moerlein place consisted of a 189-acre farm on Port Union Road. This was near the Miami-Erie Canal, which ran south to the Ohio River by the Over-the-Rhine district, where the Moerlein Brewery was located, so that one could travel back and forth by means of the canal. The Moerlein summer home apparently had the appearance and décor of a lodge, complete with billiard tables and mounted buffalo and wolf heads on the walls. Also located there were paintings by local artists, such as Joseph Henry Sharp (1859–1953). Especially interesting was a gun collection of more then thirty items, including an 1873 Winchester and a German muzzle-loading shotgun.

Muhlhauser Barn in West Chester.

Moerlein Gazebo in West Chester.

Spring Grove Cemetery

19. Moerlein Family Burial Site
Location: Spring Grove Cemetery, Section 37
4521 Spring Grove Avenue

The Moerlein family monument is located at Spring Grove Cemetery. This beautiful landscaping masterpiece was designed by Adolph Strauch (1822–83), who served as its superintendent from 1859 until his death.[2]

Footstone for Christian Moerlein.
May 13, 1818, to May 14, 1897.

Footstone for Barbara Moerlein.
April 20, 1827, to January 6, 1903.

Cincinnati Riverfront

20. Moerlein Lager House
Location: Banks of the Ohio River

Opened on Monday, 27 February 2012, the Moerlein Lager House features the Beer Barons Hall of Fame honoring the well-known beer barons of the area. Located on the banks of the Ohio River, it overlooks the Roebling Suspension Bridge.

CHAPTER 14

Timeline of Christian Moerlein and His Namesake Brewing Company

From Inception to the Opening of the Moerlein Lager House

THE FOLLOWING TIMELINE CONSISTS OF INFORMATION compiled by the Christian Moerlein Brewing Company and brings together the basic dates, facts, and events relating to Christian Moerlein and his brewery, as well as the new Christian Moerlein Brewing Company. It is added here as a convenient reference guide to the history of both companies and shows the continuity of the Moerlein tradition.

1818. Christian Moerlein is born on 13 May 1818, the son of a blacksmith, Conrad Moerlein, in the village of Truppach, Bavaria. During his teenage years living on his family's modest farm, Christian Moerlein spends summers working as a blacksmith's apprentice and winters working at his uncle's brewery.

1836. Christian Moerlein completes his apprenticeships. He sharpens his skills for five years as a traveling journeyman working in German breweries and blacksmith shops. The knowledge he acquires during this period will serve him immensely in his later years.

1841. Seeking economic advancement, the twenty-three-year-old

Christian Moerlein boards a ship outside of Bremen, Germany, bound for America. The crossing is stormy and troublesome, taking fifty-eight days to reach Baltimore, Maryland. Moerlein arrives with just twelve dollars in his pocket.

In search of the American dream, Moerlein works as a blacksmith in Pittsburgh, Pennsylvania, then Wheeling, West Virginia, and later Portsmouth, Ohio, before finally landing steady work at a Hendricks-burg, Ohio, distillery, earning seven dollars per month.

1842. Hoping to improve his situation, Christian Moerlein arrives in Cincinnati on the first day of April. He works for seven months then uses his modest savings to open a smithy on Findlay Street and later a second location on Elm Street.

1853. By the 1850s, Moerlein is prospering as a blacksmith and as German immigrants flood into Cincinnati, the demand for good beer becomes strong. In 1853, Moerlein establishes a small brewery with Adam Dillmann on Elm Street to brew beer for local demand. Dillmann passes away in 1854, and Conrad Windisch becomes Moerlein's partner.

Moerlein's small brewery grows quickly—especially after lager beer is introduced in 1855. Pasteurization, the introduction of bottles, the Port of Cincinnati, and the railroad allow Moerlein to ship his beers to distant markets.

1866. Moerlein buys out Conrad Windisch, who then partners with Heinrich and Gottlieb Muhlhauser to form the Lion Brewery, later known as the Windisch-Muhlhauser Brewing Company.

1876. Through the efforts of Christian's son George, Moerlein beers are introduced at the U.S. Centennial Exposition in Philadelphia. An ardent promoter of his family's beers, George Moerlein once rode on horseback in and out of the many Vine Street saloons ordering his beer to the amusement of patrons.

1880s. Christian Moerlein Brewing Company is an early beer industry proponent of advertising. The company introduces some of the most attractive and effective advertising pieces of the day. Moerlein ads often boast of awards received at various expositions of the period. Gold medals and blue ribbons at 1800s industrial expositions were the equivalent of modern-day awards at events like the Great American Beer Festival or World Beer Cup.

1890. Christian Moerlein becomes a partner in a second brewery in Nashville, Tennessee, known as the Moerlein-Gerst Brewing Company. Like the Cincinnati brewery, Moerlein-Gerst utilizes crock bottles similar to those used in Cincinnati. Moerlein sells his interest and the brewery becomes the William Gerst Brewing Company in 1893.

1895. Christian Moerlein beers represent the hallmark of quality and are "crowned wherever exhibited" with the highest awards. Cincinnatians drink more beer per capita than any other city in the country: more than forty gallons per person!

1897. Christian Moerlein dies at the age of seventy-nine on 14 May. At the time of his death the Moerlein Brewing facility encompasses three city blocks on Elm Street, near Findlay Market, including a bottling department, offices, stables, and vast lager cellars. Christian Moerlein Brewing Company is recognized as the largest brewery in Cincinnati and the state of Ohio. His sons continue the business with the same traditions of quality as their father.

1900. At the turn of the century, Christian Moerlein Brewing Company continues with great success and is among the largest in the nation. Moerlein beers have gained a national reputation and are commonly exported to Central America, Puerto Rico, and Europe.

1901. National brands begin "exporting" their beers into the Cincinnati market from Saint Louis and Milwaukee. While these brands are experimenting with national growth, Cincinnati brewers are selling all they can make locally and, therefore, have little interest in marketing their beer across the country. This hesitancy to expand into outside markets would contribute to the eventual downfall of the Cincinnati beer industry as national brands begin making inroads against the local Cincinnati brewers later in the century.

1910. The Barbarossa brand became a mainstay in the Christian Moerlein beer portfolio. The packaging features Frederick I, Emperor of the Holy Roman Empire of the German Nation, on the label. The Barbarossa brand proved so popular that it actually survived Prohibition while the Moerlein brewery did not. Red Top Brewing Company revived the Barbarossa brand several years after the repeal of Prohibition. Today, Barbarossa continues as a mainstay of the Moerlein line up, with branding similar to the labels one hundred years prior.

1912. Christian Moerlein beers feature colorful advertisement material on signs and other point-of-sale items they supplied to area bars. Old men are often featured in these "ads" to promote the image of a wise, older individual who should know a good beer when he drinks one and women to counter the growing temperance movement of the time.

1919. As Prohibition draws near, Christian Moerlein Brewing Company is the largest brewery in Ohio and ninth largest in the United States, with an annual capacity of more than a half million barrels. The company is an early pioneer in shipping kegs to bottlers around the nation who then bottled the beer for local distribution. Moerlein beers were bottled in cities such as New York, Philadelphia, Boston, Atlantic City, and Los Angeles and the labels listed the local bottlers.

Prohibition forces the end of beer deliveries by April 1919 and following poor sales of "Chrismo" a near beer, the Christian Moerlein Brewing Company suspends operations.. After the final closing of the Elm Street office in 1924, the celebrated Moerlein beers seem to be lost forever in history.

1933. At the end of Prohibition, the Christian Moerlein Brewing Company was rumored to revive its brewing operations with a planned new facility on Paddock Road near Tennessee Avenue. Though the revival was met with great anticipation, brewing operations never resumed.

1981. Hudepohl Brewing Company, under the leadership of Bob Pohl, reintroduces the Christian Moerlein name to Cincinnati beer drinkers in the form of a "craft," Reinheitsgebot pure beer formulated by Hudepohl brewmaster, Gerry Erftenbeck, using recipes and knowledge from brewing a century earlier. Christian Moerlein Select Lager makes its debut on 14 September as a "Better Beer" before the widely recognized "Craft Beer" category of today. The recipe proves a great success and for a time, the Hudepohl Brewery cannot keep up with demand for the new beer. Hudepohl doesn't know it, but it is ahead of its time as Christian Moerlein helps pave the way for future microbrews and is considered a pioneer brand of today's craft beer movement.

1982. Hudepohl introduces Christian Moerlein Select Lager in cans. At first, the cans are only for those accounts where glass bottles are prohibited, but by 1984 the cans are being sold at most Greater Cincinnati retail accounts. Moerlein becomes one of the first craft beers sold in cans.

1984. A huge milestone is achieved and history is made on 13 January when Christian Moerlein Select Lager is certified by the German VLB in Berlin as the first American beer to pass Germany's Reinheitsgebot Purity Law, enacted in 1516. The law states that all beers sold in Germany can contain only four ingredients: Yeast, barley malt, hops and water. It was later amended to include wheat. This achievement means that Christian Moerlein is the first American beer that can be sold in Germany.

1992. Hudepohl-Schoenling repackages the Christian Moerlein brand, changing the name to Moerlein's Cincinnati Select Lager. The idea is to highlight the beers authentic craft character and reposition Moerlein into the now fast-growing craft beer category.

Christian Moerlein Bock Beer is released. The beer was first brewed in the late nineteenth century. Cincinnati's inaugural Bockfest is planned by the now-merged Hudepohl-Schoenling Brewing Company to coincide with the product launch of Moerlein's Cincinnati Bock.

1996. Hudepohl-Schoenling sells its Central Parkway facility to Boston Beer Company. All brewing continues for Cincinnati's great beer brands under a production agreement with Boston Beer.

1997. Hudepohl-Schoenling opens a new microbrewery in August, adjacent to the company's keg dock at 1648 Central Avenue. The new brewery makes many new interesting recipes. Christian Moerlein Honey Almond is introduced and promptly wins a gold medal at the 1997 World Beer Championships.

1998. Christian Moerlein Select Lager is named "World Champion Munich-Helles style lager," at the World Beer Championships. It tops some of the best-known brands from the USA and around the world including Germany and the Netherlands.

1999. The Hudepohl-Schoenling Brewing Company and all its brands, including Christian Moerlein, Hudepohl, Hudy Delight, Hudy 14-K, Burger, Schoenling, and Little Kings Cream Ale are sold to the Snyder International Brewing Group headquartered in Cleveland, Ohio, and later having brewing operations in Frederick, Maryland.

2001. The Boston Beer Company production agreement to brew Cincinnati's great beer brands in Cincinnati ends and the contract is not renewed; ending a great era in Cincinnati's brewing history. All production of Cincinnati's great beer brands, including Christian Moerlein are now done in out-of-town breweries. The Snyder International Brewing Group maintains a single office in the Cincinnati suburb of Blue Ash, where the Hudepohl-Schoenling Brewing Company resides.

2002. The Snyder International Brewing Group is forced to shut down the local Hudepohl-Schoenling Brewing Company satellite office, caused by slimming sales in part due to a lack of local brewing and ownership for Cincinnati's great beer brands. Some personnel are transferred to the Snyder's Frederick, Maryland, facility and the company files for court-ordered receivership protection.

2004. Beer industry veteran and greater Cincinnati resident Gregory S. Hardman is introduced as the new owner of Christian Moerlein Brewing Company, promising to return the grand brewing traditions that once made Cincinnati a brewing mecca in the nineteenth and twentieth centuries. Hardman quickly devises a four-phase plan in order to do accomplish this.

- Return local ownership of Cincinnati's great beer brands.
- Reposition the brands by highlighting each brand's authenticity making them relevant to today's consumers in order to build sales and eventually open local brewing operations.
- Return brewing to Cincinnati and open a Christian Moerlein production brewery in Cincinnati's Over-the-Rhine Brewery District.
- Open a world-class Christian Moerlein Lager House on the banks of the Ohio River in Cincinnati Riverfront Park.

2006. With the purchase of the Christian Moerlein brand two years earlier, Hardman negotiates a right of first refusal on many of the great Cincinnati beer brands once owned by Hudepohl-Schoenling. Hardman exercises his first right of refusal as owner of Christian Moerlein Brewing Company and gains control of more than sixty Cincinnati brands, except for the Little Kings brand which he has distribution rights only. Hardman re-establishes the Hudepohl-Schoenling Brewing Company under the ownership of Christian Moerlein

Brewing Company and begins his quest to relaunch Cincinnati's great beer brands.

2007. After stabilizing the Christian Moerlein brand, Hardman introduces the first new Moerlein beer in over a decade—Moerlein O.T.R. (Over-the-Rhine Ale), a pale ale based on an early settler's recipe with generous amounts of hops and a full malt character. O.T.R. is an immediate success, leading the way for additional handcrafted brews from Moerlein lagers and ales.

2008. The success of the Moerlein brands paves the way for the relaunch of Cincinnati's great beer brands. On 30 October, Hudy Delight is relaunched with a new can commemorating the thirtieth anniversary of the brand. Hardman, through his Hudepohl-Schoenling subsidiary ends the year by announcing the acquisition of the Little Kings brand on 31 December 2008. Within months, Little Kings is rebranded with graphics paying tribute to its former greatness, including adding the Schoenling brewery name to the logo.

2009. In May, Burger Classic is relaunched at the Cincinnati Reds Hall of Fame and Museum exhibit honoring Crosley Field, where the beer was once sold. Within hours of the opening, fans are lined around the block to catch a glimpse of the Burger Beer cans.

Hudy 14-K cans make their way back to Cincinnati shelves in September. The launch is quickly followed by the introduction of both Hudy 14-K and Hudy Delight six-pack bottles.

In September, Christian Moerlein Brewing Company and the Cincinnati Park Board announce plans for the development of the Moerlein Lager House in Cincinnati Riverfront Park later to be named Phyllis W. Smale Riverfront Park.

With plans for the Moerlein Lager House well under way, Hardman announces in April, plans to develop the former Husman Potato Chip factory and Kauffman pre-Prohibition brewery as the new Christian Moerlein Brewery in Over-the-Rhine's Brewery District. Local brewing for Cincinnati's great beer brands is on the horizon.

2010. As a tribute to Ludwig Hudepohl II being the first Cincinnati-born beer baron, and the 125th anniversary of the Hudepohl Brewing Company, Hardman launches Hudepohl Amber Lager to great success.

The end of the year marks a new chapter in Christian Moerlein history as the first Christian Moerlein Brewing Company beer is brewed in Over-the-Rhine's Brewery District since 1919. The beer is brewed to honor the 150th anniversary of Arnold's Bar & Grill, Cincinnati's oldest continually operating saloon.

2011. Construction of the new Moerlein Lager House begins in March on the Jacob G. Schmidlapp Event Lawn in Phyllis W. Smale Riverfront Park.

Hardman announces the development of the Beer Baron and Brewers Hall of Fame at the Moerlein Lager House in association with the Over-the-Rhine Brewery District Community Urban Redevelopment Corporation as a means to recognize and celebrate great brewers and preserve their history.

2012. Greg Hardman's four-phase plan and promise to return Cincinnati's great brewing traditions are realized as the Moerlein Lager House opens its doors with a Grand Opening Gala on Saturday, 25 February, where Hardman proclaims, "To the citizens of Cincinnati and the World, I present to you the Christian Moerlein Lager House."

Appendix A

Fellow Beer Barons

AS THE MAJOR BEER BARON of the Over-the-Rhine district, Christian Moerlein, no doubt, had to interact with other beer barons of the area on a regular basis. Of them, he probably had the closest business and community relationships with four of them: Daniel Jung, Conrad Windisch, and Gottlieb and Heinrich Mühlhäuser. Jung's brother Philipp married Magdalena Oeh, the sister of Moerlein's wife, and their son J. George Jung became part of the Moerlein Brewing Company's management team. Conrad Windisch was Moerlein's business partner and the latter two were members of the Philippus Church on McMicken Avenue, which the Moerlein family also belonged to.

Additionally, the author has also translated the biography of John Kauffman, since the present-day Moerlein Brewing Company on Moore Street is housed in what was part of the Kauffman Brewing Company. Although he most likely knew Moerlein, there is no indication of the two having the kinds of relationships that the other brewers had with him. Nevertheless, it is interesting to compare and contrast his life story as well as the other beer barons covered here with that of Moerlein, as there are many similarities to be found among them.

Daniel Jung (1822–77)
From *Der Deutsche Pionier*

Daniel Jung was born 11 February 1822 in Haschbach [aka Remigius-berg] near Cusel in the Bavarian Palatinate, where his parents, Philipp and Margarethe, were farmers. At age fifteen, he and a cousin named Kreuz came to America. They landed in New York in March 1837, from whence Kreuz went directly to a farm in the east that he had purchased or leased, leaving his young cousin to his own devices in New York without any contacts at all and supplied only with the barest of necessities. Jung succeeded in making his way to Buffalo, where he found a position as an apprentice with a German blacksmith and learned the trade there for a period of three years. As a journeyman blacksmith he then moved to Akron, where he worked for a year at establishing his own business, then moving on to Cincinnati in 1841. There the barely twenty year old young man found work as a journeyman blacksmith with Peter König in what was then Hamilton Road (now McMicken Avenue).

Jung was soon taken on as a partner due to the fact that he was so hardworking, remaining with König until 1846. He then longed to see his loved ones in the old country and so took a trip home to Germany. After getting engaged with a cousin, Philippine Jung, who soon followed him to America, Jung returned to Cincinnati with his three brothers in the summer of 1847 by way of New Orleans. While on the steamboat trip, they unfortunately suffered a shipwreck near Shreveport, Louisiana, when the ship hit a reef, causing it to sink in a matter of minutes, so that the Jungs lost almost everything. The courageous behavior of Jung, who immediately dived into the Mississippi, caused others to do likewise, so that none of the German immigrants on board were swallowed up by the Father of Waters.

With great difficulty they climbed up onto the reef and had to wait there for twenty-four hours—a terribly dark night was followed by a burning hot day—until they were picked up by a steamer headed for Cincinnati. When they arrived at their destination, they were, of

Daniel Jung

course, empty handed. At the time of the shipwreck, Jung had forty dollars in his pockets, but which was soon expended to provide for the needs of himself and his brothers on the trip to Cincinnati. So they arrived completely broke, but Jung already had established a solid reputation in the area, so that in a few months we find him as a blacksmith master craftsman on Central Avenue. In 1848 his fiancé arrived and they were soon married; she passed away in March 1864. Together they had eight children, three of which are still among us.

In 1854 Jung joined Peter Weyand, an experienced beer brewer, in establishing a brewery on the site of his blacksmith shop under the name Weyand and Jung. At first, they only brewed top-fermented beer, which was known as "common beer," the first brew being completed in October 1855. Initially, they were limited in what they could produce due to means at their disposal, but they worked hard at their business and after three years expanded their produce to include lager beer.

By 1866 their business had expanded to such an extent that they acquired land on Freeman Avenue, where they built a more extensive brewing facility with room for thirty thousand barrels of beer. Their company is still known as the Western Brewery. Unfortunately, their company hit on the hard times that oppressed business and industry in the West and the company went into bankruptcy, whereupon Weyand passed away. Gradually, Jung was able to lift the brewery out of its financial woes and pay off its debts.

Sadly, Jung was not able to witness the complete recovery of his business and the payment of all of its creditors. He had suffered for many years from rheumatism and on 2 December suffered a fatal heart attack. He was survived by his second wife, the widow Catharina Heintz, née Weissmann; a son, Daniel; two daughters, Catharina and Anna Jung; as well as two stepdaughters, Mrs. König and Miss Heintz. At the time of his death, he belonged to several societies, including the Brewers Association, the German Pioneer Society (a member since its founding) and other societies as well. He was a member of the German Protestant Saint John's Church on Elm Street.

As an untiring businessman, who maintained his integrity in spite of a vexatious fate, as a generous citizen and helpful friend, as well as a true German in the best sense of the word, Jung had a great circle of friends and the huge attendance at his funeral testifies to the high regard in which he was held.[1]

[Source: Translated by the author from "Daniel Jung," *Der Deutsche Pionier* 9 (1878): 452–53]

Conrad Windisch (1825–87)
From *Cincinnati in Wort und Bild*
by Max Burgheim

There is absolutely no question that Conrad Windisch has to be considered one of the pioneers of the brewing industry in America. He was born 6 March 1825 in Egloffstein in Bavaria, the son of Ulrich Windisch, the owner of a brewery, and received a meager education in the elementary school of his hometown. Fortunately, his formal education was greatly supplemented in his parental home, as well as by later experiences in life.

By the age of thirteen, the time for study was over, as his father needed help in the brewery and on the farm. And, since he was a strong lad, he had to work very hard at both of them. When he was twenty-three his father passed away, so that he now had to take on the responsibility of helping run the brewery and farm to support the family. By this time, he had become quite competent in both areas as a result of having learned both trades under the watchful eye of his father.

Then came the fateful year of 1848 that drove so many Germans across the ocean to America and which awakened the desire in him to immigrate. Since prospects for the future did not seem all that promising in the fatherland, he decided to immigrate to America and bid farewell to his family. On 1 November 1848, he boarded a sailing vessel for the journey to America, with the ship finally arriving in New York on 1 February 1849 after a turbulent voyage lasting three months.

Without remaining long in this Gotham, which was so dangerous for recently arrived immigrants, Windisch immediately took a coach to Pittsburgh. The journey over the Alleghenies during a relatively harsh winter was just as difficult as the ocean voyage to America had been. However, his adventurous spirit, energy, and strong constitution helped him through it all.

In Pittsburgh he hoped to find work and finally found a job at a small brewery with a salary of five dollars per month, but which also provided him with room and board. In spite of the poor salary he held onto the job, hoping his pay would increase. And by means of hard work it actually did increase after a few months to six and then to seven dollars a month. However, he eventually got fed up with the poor salary, so he and three other young Germans took a canal boat to Erie, and from there to Chicago, and then on to Saint Louis in the hopes of finding better-paying jobs.

However, his hopes did not come to fruition and so without thinking any further, he made his way across the Mississippi River to Belleville, Illinois, where he found a job at a brewery for eleven dollars per month. But it was a miserable place with a beer cellar that had been a coal mine. He worked in damp and musty quarters day and night with the result that he got sick with fever. He, therefore, had no choice, but to find another job with conditions more conducive to his health. After recovering from fever, he returned to Saint Louis, where he found a job at the Camp Spring Brewery. But this also was not to his liking, so he decided to move to Cincinnati with what savings he had left, as he had friends and acquaintances there. In Cincinnati he not only found them, but also a good job in the Herancourt Brewery as well.[2]

His new job was actually just what he was looking for. After working there for about eight months, his abilities as a brewer became well known and he was able to get a better position at Koehler's Buckeye Brewery. There he swiftly rose to the position of Braumeister.[3] He held this quite responsible and relatively well-paid position for a period of three years, which enabled him to save up a tidy some of money as well. Additionally, Windisch also received his family inheritance at this time, so that his entire savings amounted to about eighteen hundred dollars. From now on, Windisch was clearly on the road to success.

At around this time Christian Moerlein's brewery partner, Adam Dillmann, had passed away and he, therefore, had need of a competent and experienced brewer to take his place. So he got together with Windisch, forming a business partnership in 1854 that lasted till 1866.

KREBS LITHO. CO. CINCINNATI.

Conrad Windisch

During this time, their brewery acquired a great reputation and did quite well financially, especially as a result of its lager beer.

In 1866, Windisch dissolved his association with Moerlein, who bought him out for a quite substantial sum of money, and established the Löwen-Brauerei/Lion Brewery together with Gottlieb and Heinrich Mühlhäuser. Their brewery became well known as one of the best breweries in the United States, with Windisch contributing greatly to its outstanding reputation and financial success.

In 1854 Conrad Windisch married Sophie Wilhelmine Kobmann who was from his hometown (Egloffstein, Bavaria) and their happy marriage was blessed with seven children, of which five are still alive at the time of this writing [1888]. The oldest son, Johann U. F. Windisch, who married Louise Müller, serves as secretary of the company. Windisch's two other sons, William A. and Charles F., are also involved in the brewery as well. The oldest daughter, Pauline, is married to John C. Schwarz in Hamilton, Ohio, and the younger daughter is still at home. As a result of several strokes, which left him partially incapacitated, Windisch passed away 2 July 1887. His impressive funeral bore witness to the respect and admiration this honorable man enjoyed in the city of Cincinnati.

[Translated by the author from Max Burgheim, *Cincinnati in Wort und Bild* (Cincinnati: M. & R. Burgheim, 1888).]

Gottlieb Mühlhäuser (1836–1905
From *Cincinnati in Wort und Bild*
by Max Burgheim

In 1840, the Friedrich Mühlhäuser family left its home town of Muggendorf in Bavaria and immigrated to America. After arriving in the United States, the family headed west, settling down on a farm in the vicinity of Portsmouth, Ohio. Here they led a life that left much to be desired. So dissatisfied were they with circumstances there that after a period of five years, they moved to Cincinnati. By that time, it already had an ever increasing German element and Friedrich Mühlhäuser felt that it offered more promising prospects for the future of the family than remaining on the farm. Soon after moving to Cincinnati, he opened a grocery store on Hamilton Road [now McMicken Avenue] in the Over-the-Rhine district.

His eldest son, Gottlieb Mühlhäuser, was only five years old when the family came to America and was, of course, not old enough to be of much help. Indeed, he was in need of education at this time, so he attended the Buckeye School and later on the school directed by Professor Hoferich in the Washington Park area in the Over-the-Rhine district.

In 1848 the family suffered a heavy blow with the death of their father. The responsibility of caring for the family now fell to the mother. Gottlieb was thirteen at the time and had to leave school to help earn money for the support of the family. His first job was at a pottery on Freeman Street. The circumstances surrounding apprenticeship were not that good then; a youth like Gottlieb earned a salary that was at best barely at today's subsistence level even if you were hardworking and industrious. However, food was cheaper then and the purchasing power of money greater as well.

The young pottery apprentice earned $1.50 per week. We can only imagine, but not describe his feelings when he first brought home his earnings and placed them in the hands of his mother. After working hard for some time on this job and earning the respect of his boss, the opportunity presented itself of earning more elsewhere. He, therefore, accepted a position at Anton Ritter's mineral water factory on Vine Street. This job appealed to him from the start. At the time, he had no idea that this job would lay the foundations for his future success in life.

He worked with Ritter till 1854 and, although he gave almost all of his income to his mother for the support of the family, he did manage to save up a total of ninety dollars due to his thriftiness. As a result of this and his enterprising spirit, he got the idea of starting his own mineral water factory. All went well with this new venture and business was so good that he was able to open a branch in Chillicothe in 1855 and two years later another one in Hamilton. Around this time, his brother Heinrich had come of age, so he took him on as a business partner in the company. Both worked exceedingly well together and were also exceptionally energetic in building up their company. They also had a knack for making friends and seemed to be successful in whatever they did.

In 1859 they sold the mineral water factory and acquired a flour mill, which they transformed into one powered by steam. This business proved also to be quite successful and orders increased daily, so that they found it necessary to expand the size of the operation. It reached its zenith during the Civil War when the mill produced 150–200 barrels of flour daily (at the time a rather substantial amount). Almost all of the produce went directly to the federal government due to the demands caused by the war, earning great profits for the brothers as a result.

A few years after the Civil War, they decided to sell the mill and establish a brewery. This decision came about after they got together with Conrad Windisch, a competent and experienced brewer who had been in partnership with Christian Moerlein. Together, they established the Löwen-Brauerei/Lion Brewery. Early on, it operated on a rather small scale, but due to its excellent beer and the extraordinary energy the three put into selling their product, the brewery soon not only competed with other breweries, but surpassed them in terms of production as well.

The brewery's first cellar was built in 1866 and right on the spot where part of the brewery is located today and was where an iron foundry had previously been located. In 1867 the building that now forms the upper wing of the brewery was constructed and in 1868/69, the southern cellars and the lower wing of the brewery were built. The building on the corner of Wade and Plum Streets was constructed later on, in 1887/88.

In the course of time, this great brewery not only earned an enviable name in the city of Cincinnati and the state of Ohio, but also beyond their borders as well. As soon as the brewery opened, Gottlieb learned the art of brewing from Windisch and, being an intelligent student of the trade, soon became its Braumeister.

In 1857 he married Christine Windisch, a sister of the now departed Conrad Windisch and daughter of Ulrich Windisch of Egloffstein, Bavaria. They had six children, five of whom are still alive at the time of this writing [1888]. Both sons, Heinrich and Eduard, are occupied in the brewery, and show promise of following in the footsteps of their father. Heinrich, Jr., married Ellen Schlemmer in 1883, while the oldest daughter, Mathilde, married Eduard Lapp. Both marriages have brought forth grandchildren, something that brought great joy to the grandparents. Both of the youngest daughters are still

KREBS LITHO. CO. CINCINNATI.

G. Mühlhäuser

with their parents.

Since the death of Windisch in 1887, Gottlieb Mühlhäuser has served as president of the brewery, as well as its technical director. He calmly and skillfully directs the brewery and its tremendous success is due mainly to him. He is held in high esteem in the community at large, as might be expected of someone with such an impeccable character as his.

[Translated by the author from Max Burgheim, *Cincinnati in Wort und Bild* (Cincinnati: M. & R. Burgheim, 1888).]

Heinrich Mühlhäuser (1842–1914)
From *Cincinnati in Wort und Bild*
by Max Burgheim

After the Mühlhäuser family came to America in 1840 and settled on a farm near Portsmouth, Ohio, a second son, Heinrich, was born. As noted earlier, the family then moved to Cincinnati in 1845, where the father opened a grocery store on Hamilton Road (now McMicken Avenue) in the Over-the-Rhine district. At the time of the father's death in 1848, Heinrich was only six years old, so that his upbringing fell on his mother's shoulders, as did running the store. Heinrich attended public school till he was eleven and then left, so he could help out at the store.

As a boy, he developed a keen sense for business affairs, joining his elder brother as a partner in the mineral water business after his mother had retired. Both brothers worked well together and went on to establish a flour mill, which proved to be just as successful, earning them great profits.

After selling the mill in 1866, they joined Conrad Windisch in establishing the Löwen-Brauerei/Lion Brewery, with Heinrich taking on the responsibility of heading up the department for public relations, a position for which he was well suited. He soon emerged as one of the major pillars of the brewery. Whoever saw him at work, knows how greatly in demand he is and how he daily has to answer all kinds of questions, so that we can't help but be amazed at the patience and tact he displays in everything he does.

He has also taken an active a role in public affairs, where he is as diligent and accomplished as he is in business matters. It is, therefore, not surprising that he is in great demand as a representative of the citizenry of the area and serves on the boards of many institutions and organizations.

Heinrich Mühlhäuser probably won the greatest of his laurel wreaths of honor in the battle against the temperance movement of the state of Ohio. His activities in this battle have earned him the

KREBS LITHO.CO. CINCINNATI.

Heinrich   Mühlhäuser

respect and honor of all open-minded people in the German- and Anglo-American communities. The fanatical temperance movement in our state had long since been a well organized one, without the liberal-minded people of Ohio ever having the slightest notion that such fanatics would ever be able to gain the upper hand in their endeavors. However, all of a sudden the proponents of temperance succeeded in gaining the majority in the state legislature, with the result that laws were passed limiting our personal liberty.

In response to these developments, the open-minded people of Ohio now got organized, especially in the larger cities of the state, earnestly taking on the battle to regain our rights.[2] They found an ideal leader in Heinrich Mühlhäuser, in whom they placed their trust in this long fought out battle, knowing that with him they had the best chance of success. He proved that their trust was completely justified and the results attained were due mainly to his unswerving resolve, untiring energy, and his firm belief in the principles of personal liberty.

Although born in this country, Heinrich Mühlhäuser is thoroughly German from head to toe, and is actively involved in community affairs. The German societies have found him to be one of their strongest supporters, as well as an active community leader and there is hardly a German affair in the area that does not find him among its participants.

In 1869, Heinrich Mühlhäuser married Maria Schmidt and they have five children (two boys and three girls), all of whom have received the greatest attention with regard to their upbringing and bring great joy to the family.[4]

[Translated by the author from Max Burgheim, *Cincinnati in Wort und Bild* (Cincinnati: M. & R. Burgheim, 1888).]

John Kauffman (1830–86)
From *Cincinnati und sein Deutschthum*

John Kauffman [note: originally Kauffmann] contributed greatly to the reputation Cincinnati enjoys worldwide of brewing the best beer in North America. And even if he is no longer with us, having passed away 15 January 1886, he has certainly not been forgotten.

John Kauffman was born 10 February 1830 in Kurviller in Lorraine, now part of the German province of Alsace-Lorraine, where he learned German and French in school. At age fifteen, he immigrated to America, going directly to Cincinnati, where he found work at the Franklin Brewery of his uncle John Kauffmann, which was located near Deer Creek. Initially, he was simply a worker there, but in time advanced to the position of malter, eventually becoming foreman. He remained in this position for four years until his uncle passed away.

Under his direction the Ohio Brewery was then established with

KREBS LITHO.CO. CINCINNATI.

John Kauffman

him serving as foreman for a short time until he took a position as foreman at the Jefferson Brewery of August Tiemann. Later, he became foreman for the brewery of George F. Eichenlaub in Walnut Hills, a position he held for four years. Together with Eichenlaub and Rudolph Rheinbold he then took over the Franklin Brewery that had belonged to his uncle and where his career had begun.

Another four years went by until the firm of Kauffman and Company was formed in 1859. Construction began that year on the brew-

Kauffman Felsenkeller

ery on Vine Street and was completed in 1860, the year in which brewing began there. During construction of the brewery, Kauffman acquired the grist mill on Walnut Street (now the well-known Schneider mill), trying his luck as a miller.

However, he remained loyal to Gambrinus, the patron saint of beer and brewing, and only ran the mill on the side. In 1865 Eichenlaub left the brewery, which was now run by Kauffman and Rheinbold. In April 1877 the latter left the company, so that Kauffman alone was in charge of the brewery.

Kauffman was married to Marianne Eichenlaub, the daughter of George F. Eichenlaub, and they had nine children, of which two sons are still alive.[5]

[Source: Translated by the author from *Cincinnati und sein Deutschthum: Eine Geschichte der Entwickelung Cincinnati's und seines Deutschthums, mit biographischen Skizzen und Illustrationen* (Cincinnati: Queen City Publishing Co., 1901).]

❖

Cut from the Same Cloth

Although they were competitors in the same industry, Cincinnati's beer barons not only lived relatively close together, but also had much in common. Like Moerlein, they and their families were motivated to come to America by the promise of a better life and realizing the American Dream. Each of them is worth a closer look with regard to the image that emerges of them. Here we want to focus on Jung, Windisch, and the Mühlhäuser brother, leaving Kauffman aside as his inclusion here relates to the present-day Moerlein Brewing Company.

Jung is described as "hard working" and as "an untiring businessman" who established a "solid reputation in the area." He also was held "in high regard" and considered "a true German in the best sense of the word." Due to the young age at which he emigrated from Bavaria to America, he obviously was imbued with the spirit of ambition and getting ahead in the New World. Additionally, he belonged to various societies and his family belonged to the German Protestant Saint John's Church on Elm Street.

Windisch is described by Burgheim "as one of the pioneers of the brewing industry in America." Sociopolitical conditions definitely played a role in causing him to come to America, as Burgheim makes reference to the 1848 Revolution: "The fateful year of 1848, which drove so many from Germany across the ocean to America, awakened within him the desire to immigrate and, as the prospects for a happy future in his homeland didn't seem to be the best, he swiftly decided to bid farewell to his fatherland and on 1 November 1848 boarded a sailing vessel to America."

Upon arrival in America, he found employment at a brewery: "In spite of the low salary he held on to the job in the hope that it would increase and by means of hard work his salary did increase." Here the theme of hard work and persistence are highlighted as the key to Windisch's success story. He is also referred to as "a competent and experienced brewer" who "contributed greatly to the enormous reputation and great financial success" of the Lion Brewery.

The importance of friends and family are also emphasized. His reasons for coming to Cincinnati are similar to those of Moerlein: "he decided to move to Cincinnati with what savings he had, as he had friends and acquaintances there, in order to possibly find a better position."

Burgheim writes that Windisch was from Egloffstein. This was a village located not that far from Moerlein's hometown of Truppach. And like Moerlein, he also had a large family, with three of his sons involved in the brewery. He also writes that the Mühlhäuser family came from the nearby village of Muggendorf and that both brothers raised large families and that their sons were also involved in their brewery.

Burgheim stresses that Gottlieb Mühlhäuser was noted for his hard work and that this was "the foundation for his future success." He also notes his thrift and the energy he brought to whatever he did. Additionally, "Both brothers worked well together with an admirable amount of energy. Also, they knew how to make friends and were successful at everything they did."

Heinrich Mühlhäuser is described as having "a keen sense for business matters" and was well known for his "patience and tact." Not surprisingly, he was "a much sought after representative by the citizenry of the area" and served "on the boards of many institutions." He was also actively involved in community affairs and Burgheim writes that "there is no German affair that takes place in which he is not actively involved in some significant way."

The similarities between Jung, Windisch, the Mühlhäuser brothers, and Moerlein are striking. Their families all originated in Bavaria, with Jung coming from the Bavarian Palatinate and the others from Upper Franconia. Today, half of the breweries in Germany are located in the state of Bavaria, so all five of these brewers came from a state with a strong brewing heritage.

Here we might comment on the origins of brewers in Cincinnati. In a survey of the places of origin of forty-two brewers: twelve were from Bavaria, twelve from Northern Germany (locations north and northeast of Bavaria), eleven from Southern Germany (locations west of Bavaria), six from Alsace-Lorraine, and one from Switzerland.

Although northern and southern Germany had equally high numbers, they include various states in these regions, so that Bavaria clearly is the one single state that contributed the greatest number of brewers to Cincinnati.[6]

Brewers covered here also shared the same religious heritage of membership in the Evangelical-Lutheran Church of Bavaria, so it is not surprising that the families discussed here joined and supported churches in Over-the-Rhine that most closely approximated its theological background: German Protestant Saint John's Church on Elm Street and the Philippus Church on McMicken Avenue, both now part of the United Church of Christ. Perhaps the Protestant work ethic comes into play here, as all of these brewers were known for their hard work, thrift, and persistence, which contributed greatly to their success in the brewing industry.

Aside from their involvement in the life of their church, these brewers also took an active role in community affairs, belonging to and leading various German-American activities and societies. Additionally, they supported a wide array of philanthropic and beneficial programs, events, and activities.

It is especially noteworthy that all of the brewers had large families: eight children in the Jung family, seven in the Windisch family, six in the Gottlieb Mühlhäuser family, and five in the Heinrich Mühlhäuser family. Although not all offspring survived childhood, there were twelve children in the Moerlein family. And, even if we are not including Kauffman in this analysis, mention might be made that there were nine children in his family. Most importantly for the breweries involved is the fact that sons and sons-in-law were all involved in their companies, as well as in the community at large.

Although the biographies of the brewers covered here are not as long as Moerlein's, they clearly evidence many similarities, showing that they were "cut from the same cloth." The fact that their biographies are not as long as Moerlein's would seem to validate Moerlein's reputation as the foremost beer baron of the area. A reading of the biographies of other beer barons of the area would no doubt find many similarities with those covered here.

Appendix B

Lager Beer

ONE OF THE MAJOR GERMAN CONTRIBUTIONS to America was the introduction of lager beer in the nineteenth century. Even its name points to its German origin, with the name coming from the German verb *lagern* (to store) as this relates to the time necessary for its fermentation. Two selections are included here, first, to explain what is involved in the production of beer, and the second to trace the origins and history of lager beer. They have been added because questions often arise on both topics. Additionally, they complement this biography, since both were drawn from works published in Cincinnati.

The Manufacture of Beer
From *They Built a City*

The art of brewing is old. Beer is a beverage prepared from malted barley (rarely from malted wheat); rice, corn, or their byproducts are often added. Basically all beer is alike, although special formulas, jealously guarded give distinctive flavors to the finished brew.

The manufacture of beer involves two distinct operations—malting and brewing. Malting changes the chemical composition of the barley grains to make them soluble to water, to produce a liquid which can afterward be fermented. The brewing process converts the malt into beer. The crushed malt is extracted in hot water when the diastase completes its action in changing the starch to dextrine maltrose. After the malt has been treated, the solution is drawn off; the resulting mixture called wort, is rapidly cooled, yeast is added, and fermentation begins. Then the sugar is split into alcohol and carbonic acid gas—a process which releases a little free acid, glycerin, and aromatic bodies in small quantities. From these processes comes the beverage called beer. The brew is then placed in vats, so that it can properly age and undergo the slow process of after-fermentation and ripening. It is filtered and finally put through a completely mechanized process of barreling, bottling, or canning. Bottles, barrels and metal containers are cleaned and filled by means of immense and intricate machines; manpower merely keeps the production going.

[Source: *They Built a City: 150 Years of Industrial Cincinnati*, comp. and written by the Cincinnati Federal Writers' Project of the Works Progress Administration in Ohio (Cincinnati: The Cincinnati Post, 1938).]

Lager Beer
From *The Brewing Industry and the
Brewery Workers' Movement in America*
by Hermann Schlüter

Until the early forties of the nineteenth century, all the beer brewed in America, aside from the different kinds of small beer, was the sort known today as ale and porter. Lager beer, which had been brewed in Germany since the thirteenth century, was not known in America.

Lager beer requires slower fermentation, because it has to be brewed stronger in order to keep better. It also requires a lower temperature for its production than porter and ale. At a time, therefore, when artificial ice and cooling machines were not known and cooling places had to be provided by making cellars in the rock, the preparation of lager beer was more expensive than the other kind. In addition to this, yeast, which is necessary for the fermentation of lager beer, was not known in America; and as ships took such a long time in crossing the ocean, it was not practicable to import yeast, as it was thought that it would not keep so long.

These are probably the reasons why lager beer was not introduced into America at an earlier date, although even at that time there were large numbers of German immigrants who had made their homes in America and who were acquainted with lager beer and would surely have preferred it to that brewed according to the English method.

The exact time when lager beer, brewed according to the German method, was introduced into America is not known, nor is it certain who was the first person to brew lager beer in this country.

In Reading, Pa., there existed since 1826, a small brewery owned by a certain George Lauer, a Rhenish Bavarian, from whom it passed to his son Friedrich in 1835. This Friedrich Lauer began in 1844 or 1845 the brewing of lager beer; he explained, however, that he was not the first who introduced lager beer into America. He asserted that a certain Wagner, who had come to America in 1842, had shortly after his arrival started the brewing of lager beer in a small brewery in a suburb of Philadelphia. In the main this is substantiated by a member of the brewing firm of Engel & Wolf in Philadelphia. This gentleman says that in 1840 John Wagner brewed the first lager beer in America. This Wagner had a small brewery in John Street, near Poplar, in Philadelphia. It was a very primitive establishment in which the first lager beer of America is said to have been produced. The brewing kettle was suspended from a beam over an open fire, and this kettle contained barely eight barrels. The yeast which it is said Wagner used for this lager beer, he had sent from a brewery in Bavaria where he had formerly been brewmaster.

The great value which was placed on this lager-beer yeast can be judged from the fact that a brother-in-law of Wagner's is said to have stolen a pint of it. He was prosecuted for it and was sentenced to two years' imprisonment.

At any rate, the brewing of lager beer was developed in Philadelphia, which had in some way come into the possession of lager-beer yeast. Among the breweries which took this up was that of Engel & Wolf, in Dillwin Street, Philadelphia, which had for many years been a favorite resort of the Germans of that city who wanted to enjoy a cool drink. "More than once," it is recorded, "they drank the brewery dry," and a placard had to be put up announcing the next date when lager beer could be had. (*One Hundred Years of Brewing: A Supplement to the Western Brewer* (Chicago: H. S. Rich & Co., 1903, p. 207).

The brewing of lager beer now progressed rapidly, although in the first decade it had attained but little importance. In St. Louis a small lager-beer brewery was started as early as 1842 by Tobias Spenglar. In the city of New York the first lager beer was brewed in 1844 by George Gillig. (A German tavern keeper by the name of Schwalbe, who kept a tavern in Chatham Street, is said to have been the first to sell lager beer in New York. He had it sent from Philadelphia, and sold it at four cents a glass).

George Frey, who brewed the first lager beer in Erie, Pennsylvania, in 1847, had helped in the first brewing of "lager" in Buffalo in 1843. In 1848 a brewer in Pittsburg, John N. Straub, heard that lager beer was being brewed in Philadelphia. With great difficulty he got a quantity of lager-beer yeast from Philadelphia, which had to be brought by canal to Pittsburg, and which was used for the brewing of the first lager beer in Pittsburg.

In 1847 John A. Hauck and John Schneider started the brewing of lager beer in Chicago. In 1849 the German beverage was first produced in Cincinnati and in 1846 in Boston by John Roessle of Roxbury.

In Milwaukee the first lager beer was brewed in 1851 in the brewery of Jacob Best, out of which the Pabst establishment was later developed. Another Milwaukee brewer, a certain Wagner, it is said, had some yeast sent by his brother from Bavaria. He did not have much confidence, however, and was afraid the yeast might not be good any more. He therefore went to Best and offered him the yeast for what the transportation had cost him. Best accepted the offer. The yeast proved good, and so it came about that Jacob Best had the honor of brewing the first lager beer in Milwaukee. It is not unlikely that there is some connection between the Wagner of this story and the one who is reported to have started lager beer brewing in Philadelphia.

In the first decade after its introduction the brewing of lager beer made but slow progress in America. After this, however, with the general development of the industry, the production and consumption of the new beverage grew, and it began to replace the heavy English beers. There were economic reasons for the slowness of its development at first. Heretofore, surface-fermented beers had been used, which could be kept on tap for weeks without getting stale and unusable. Such beers were more suited for the thinly settled regions, where beer was not consumed in large quantities, but sold in glasses here and there.

With lager beer the situation was different, especially at a time when modern beer-drawing apparatus were not to be had, such as will prevent the entrance of air to the contents of the tapped barrel and thus partly prevent the carbonic acid of the beer from escaping. Lager beer is good only when freshly tapped. If it is open long it becomes stale and unusable, and therefore requires rapid consumption.

A rapid consumption of the beverage, however, can take place only where many people congregate. This was not generally the case in the first decades of lager-beer brewing in America. Only on Sundays and holidays, when Germans got together to spend their free hours, was this the case. But later, with the industrial development, larger cities grew up, which attracted great masses of people and made a rapid consumption of lager beer possible; and even in smaller places the factories brought together large numbers of workingmen, where before there had been only small shops, and thus even in small places the use of lager beer became practicable. In short, the economic development prepared the ground for the increase of the lager-beer industry. In the second decade after its appearance, the growth of the lager-

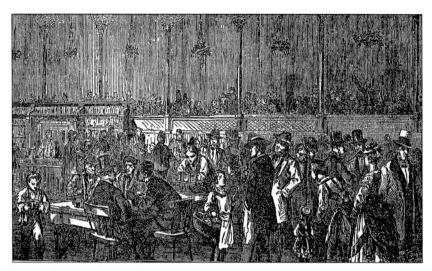

beer industry began which has lasted to our own time.

As early as 1860 far more than a quarter of the entire quantity of beer brewed in the United States was lager beer. That is, out of 3,235,545 barrels of beer, 855,803, which is far more than a quarter, were lager beer. The general economic development increased the demand for lager beer, and this increased demand naturally had an effect upon the growth and multiplication of lager-beer breweries. But the production of lager beer was limited to the winter season, because a particular temperature was necessary for manufacturing and storing it and it was difficult to obtain this temperature without artificial means. Artificial ice and artificial or mechanical cooling apparatus did not exist.

But now, as always happens when a certain need calls for a new invention, the increased demand for lager beer led to the invention of all kinds of cooling machines. The production of artificial ice, and in connection with it the building of complicated machines for manufacturing ice and producing a low temperature was greatly stimulated by the demand for lager beer. The ice industry really owes its existence to the lager-beer breweries. But the invention of cooling machines and the manufacture of artificial ice again had their effect upon the spread of the lager-beer breweries.

The brewer, who, up to that time, could manufacture his product only during certain times of the year, overcame this limitation through the use of artificial means. The natural ice, which had formerly been taken from lakes and ponds and stored in cellars, did not have to be stored underground any more, but could be kept on the ground floor or even higher, so that it had its effect from above instead of below. Natural ice was even at the beginning of the nineteenth century an article of trade between New England and New York. The natural product was shipped in great quantities from Boston to New York, where it was used for brewing purposes.

The building of icehouses began in the sixties. Improved icehouses, where, through the addition of various salts the effect of the ice was increased, began to be built in 1880, the first one in Detroit. At the same time artificial ice began to come into general use. The first ice machine in a brewery was placed in the establishment of Glasgow & Thunder, in Bendigo, Victoria, Australia, in 1860.

The first cooling machine which was used in America was introduced by the brewer, Georg Merz, in New Orleans, in 1869. He had imported it from France. In the spring of 1870, the S. Liebmann's Sons' Brewing Company in Brooklyn introduced the first cooling machine in New York or the vicinity, which was of an improved kind, but still did not meet all the requirements. The demand, however, stimulated the technicians to overcome all difficulties and to produce the perfect refrigeration machine with which today all the large breweries are equipped.

Only the development of the ice and cooling-machine industry enabled the lager-beer brewer to do away with the limits which nature had until now drawn. He did not have to brew his lager beer only at certain times of the year, but at any time when it suited him best. Human knowledge and technique had won a victory over nature.

[Source: Hermann Schlüter's *The Brewing Industry and the Brewery Workers' Movement in America* (Cincinnati, Ohio: International Union of United Brewery Workers of America, 1910).]

A Transformative Brew

Schlüter's essay was first published in 1910 and shows how the brew was brought to America in the early nineteenth century and spread throughout the country to become a major industry.[1] Its phenomenal growth and development mirrored the rise of German immigration to America. He begins by noting the difference between the British-style ales and porters, indicating that lager beer was first brewed in the thirteenth century in Germany. The former brews were popular in America due to the immigration and settlement of the colonies by people from Great Britain. They are heavier surface, or top fermented brews. These contrast with the lighter bottom fermented lager beers, which require "slower fermentation, because it has to be brewed stronger in order to keep better. It also required lower temperature for its production than porter or ale." Additionally, he notes that "yeast, which is necessary for the fermentation of lager beer, was not known in America."

Schlüter also noted that the exact date when lager beer was brewed in the United States and who brewed it is unclear. Nevertheless, he does provide some dates when lager beer was thought to have begun in various cities. Maureen Ogle updates this information in her history of brewing by noting, "For years, beer historians have credited John Wagner of Philadelphia with introducing lager to the United States, but the title of the first lager brewer probably belongs to émigrés Alexander Stausz and John Klein, who founded a tiny outfit in Alexandria, Virginia, in 1838." She also notes that "Everywhere that Germans went in the 1840s, beer flowed close at hand, and several hundred immigrant brewers opened their doors during the decade."[2] As to Cincinnati, Schlüter writes that lager beer was first brewed in 1849, Timothy J. Holian notes that reports indicate that the brew was first brewed in the 1840s and possibly even as early as 1834.[3]

What is remarkable here is how rapidly lager beer spread across the country, following in the tracks of the recent waves of the German immigration to America. As a result "production and consumption of the new beverage grew, and it began to replace the heavy English beers. . . . In the second decade after its appearance, the growth of the lager beer industry began which has lasted to our own time."

Reference is also made to the importance of lager beer in German-American social life and that the brew was especially in demand on weekends and holidays "when Germans get together to spend their free hours." Schlüter also emphasized the importance of ice and cooling machines, which "enable the lager beer brewer to do away with the limits which nature had until now drawn. He did not now have to brew his lager beer only at certain  times of the year, but at any time when it suited him best."

In conclusion, he writes that it was a German-American brewer who first introduced cooling machines in America and notes, "Human knowledge and technique had won a victory." Here we see that the German immigration had not only brought a brew, but also an industry together with a whole array of innovations to the New World and in the process had brought about the emergence of an Old World social life across the country.

Major Breweries in Greater Cincinnati

AT THE PEAK OF THE BREWING INDUSTRY before the onset of Prohibition, there were thirty-six breweries in the Greater Cincinnati area, eighteen of which were in the Over-the-Rhine district and West End in Cincinnati. Before Prohibition, there were several breweries that produced most of the beer in the area. By 1894, the following were producing 100,000 and more barrels annually.[1]

Christian Moerlein – 500,000
Hauck – 300,000
Windisch-Muhlhauser – 175,000
Jung – 175,000
Kauffman – 150,000
Gerke – 140,000
Foss-Schneider – 130,000
Buckeye (later Hudepohl) – 100,000
Wiedemann – 100,000

In 1891–92, a total of thirty-three breweries were in operation with a total output of 1,350,865 barrels, of which 600,000 barrels were exported and the rest produced for local consumption. This meant that forty gallons per capita was being consumed at that time (Greater

Cincinnati's total population then was about 500,000). After the repeal of Prohibition (1936), local breweries produced 1,512,400 barrels of beer, thereby surpassing pre-Prohibition levels.[2]

Appendix D

Related Industries

Before the advent of Prohibition, a whole array of businesses and industries were related to and supported by the brewing industry. This included saloons, restaurants, cafes, theaters, opera houses, as well as a variety of areas in the food industry, such as pickle and pretzel makers, among others. Wagon and harness makers were important and most breweries had their own stables with a fleet of horses. Two other important industrial areas were the manufacturers of barrels and the producers of brass and copper works. The following selection helps explain their relation to the brewing industry of the area. Altogether the firms discussed employed well over a thousand workers, clearly demonstrating the economic impact of brewing on the area in terms of related industries.

Manufacture of Barrels
From *History of Cincinnati and Hamilton County, Ohio*

In the village of Riverside, just outside the city limits, is found the vast plant of the Cincinnati Cooperage Company. Its buildings and extensive yards adjoin that of the Fleischmann distillery, and on the south is the broad sweep of the Ohio River and the Kentucky hills. It is a just claim made without boasting that the Cincinnati Cooperage Company is the largest concern of its kind in the world, as statistics will tell.

So great is its business that it owns vast tracts of timberland in a dozen states, from which is derived the stave and heading supply. About one thousand men are kept constantly at work in the lumber camps getting out material ready for shipment to the Riverside factory. As the company uses none but thoroughly seasoned wood, an enormous stock is kept year by year in the yards. So enormous is it that at the present time fully fifteen million pieces of staves and headings are stacked up in the Riverside yards. Averaging the length of these pieces at thirty inches each, they would, if placed end to end, reach a distance of over six thousand miles, or a quarter of the earth's circumference.

The company owns its own barges and steamboat for the transportation of material from the timber districts, which are accessible by water, though a great deal of the wood supply comes by rail. There are eight stave and heading mills located in the various forest districts owned or operated by the Cincinnati Cooperage Company. At the Riverside shops five hundred men are employed, making a total of about fourteen hundred altogether who derive wages from this great company. The full manufacturing capacity of the plant averages six thousand packages a day, an indication of the immense business done by the concern.

Brass and Copper Works
From *History of Cincinnati and Hamilton County, Ohio*

Another great manufactory, a market for whose wares has been created by the beer industry, is the copper and brass works of F. C. Deckenbach Sons' Company. These works are the oldest as well as largest in this city engaged in this line of work for distilleries and breweries. Sixty men are employed. The firm is constantly increasing its facilities and introducing new machinery.

Its specialty is the manufacture of brass and copper work for breweries, and nearly all the great breweries of Cincinnati have received their outfits from this establishment, as well as many others in adjoining states. But the product of the company is not alone confined to the city and a few adjoining states, but finds a market throughout the United States. The head of the firm admits that there are larger factories than in Cincinnati, but comparatively few, since it is claimed that there is more copper consumed here than in any other city on the continent.

[Source: *History of Cincinnati and Hamilton County, Ohio* (Cincinnati: S. B. Nelson & Co., Publishers; S. B. Nelson, J. M. Runk, 1894).]

Notes

Introduction

1. The poem by Goethe and its translation are from Thomas Mann, *Thomas Mann's Addresses Delivered at the Library of Congress*, ed. Don Heinrich Tolzmann (Oxford: Peter Lang Publishing Co., 2003), 130–31.

Chapter 1: The Self-Made Man

1. Armin Tenner, *Cincinnati Sonst und Jetzt: Eine Geschichte Cincinnati's und seiner verdienstvollen Bürger deutscher Zunge, mit biographischen Skizzen und Portrait Illustrationen* (Cincinnati: Druck von Mecklenborg & Rosenthal, 1878).

2. Ibid., 165–67.

3. Note that Tenner here emphasizes the example that Moerlein has set for others, thereby demonstrating the goal of his history as being not only to tell the history of the Cincinnati Germans, but to describe and explain how prominent individuals had attained success.

4. With German trades it is customary to learn a given trade or craft by means of the apprenticeship system, whereby one learns by working with a member of one's chosen trade. Gerhard Neumann, a past engineering executive at General Electric in Cincinnati, describes and explains this system, noting that after a given number of years as an apprentice one would have to "pass a lengthy series of tests by the craft guild. . . . No one lower than a craft *Meister* was permitted, under the law, to employ apprentices and train them." See Gerhard Neumann, *Herman the German* (New York: William Morrow and Co., 1984), 15.

5. On arrival in Bremen, one would then proceed to its nearby ocean port of Bremerhaven, from which millions of immigrants disembarked on their way to America.

Recently, a museum has opened there to document and record the history of the German immigration to America, the German Emigration Center. For further information, see *Deutsches Auswandererhaus/German Emigration Center* (Bremerhaven: Deutsches Auswandererhaus, 2006).

6. The average journey by sailing vessels could be anywhere from thirty to ninety days, depending on the prevailing weather and wind conditions. For a pictorial history of the immigration experience, see Siegrfried Stölting, *Auswanderer aus alter Zeitungsgrafik* (Lilliental: Worpsweder Verlag, 1987).

7. Immigrants usually traveled to friends and family when coming to America, and here it is important to note that Moerlein did have acquaintances in Portsmouth, Ohio. Also, the route they most likely took there, and which Moerlein also took, was to travel down the Ohio River, the favored route for immigrants and settlers on their way to Cincinnati. For further information, see Don Heinrich Tolzmann, *German Heritage Guide to the Greater Cincinnati Area*, 2nd ed., (Milford, Ohio: Little Miami Pub. Co., 2007).

8. An estimated 7,500 Cincinnatians perished as a result of the cholera epidemic of 1849–50. Many Germans who died from cholera were buried at the First German Protestant Cemetery on Reading Road near Burton Lane, and since that time "the bones of the cholera victims were not disturbed through fear that the cholera germ, which is popularly considered indestructible, would escape from the graves and ravage the city. No burials since 1882, supposedly for the same reason: digging may open avenues of escape for the dread cholera." See *The WPA Guide to Cincinnati: With a New Introduction by Zane L. Miller and a New Preface by Harry Graff* (Cincinnati: Cincinnati Historical Society, 1987), 47, 345.

9. Regarding these partners, see appendix A. For further information on their breweries, see Timothy J. Holian, *Over the Barrel: The Brewing History and Beer Culture of Cincinnati, 1800 to the Present* (St. Joseph, MO: Sudhaus Press, 2000–2001), 2 vols. See also, Robert J. Wimberg, *Cincinnati Breweries* (Cincinnati: Ohio Book Store, 1989).

Chapter 2: A Success Story

1. Max Burgheim, *Cincinnati in Wort und Bild* (Cincinnati: M. & R. Burgheim, 1888), 539.

2. See *History of Cincinnati and Hamilton County, Ohio* (Cincinnati: S. B. Nelson & Co., Publishers; S. B. Nelson, J. M. Runk, 1894), 326. For an earlier English-language biographical article on Moerlein, see the *Biographical Encylopedia of Ohio of the Nineteenth Century* (Columbus, Ohio: Galaxy Publishing Co., 1876). This article says of Moerlein "His extraordinary success is due mainly to inflexible integrity, unusual financial abilities, and a thorough knowledge of all the details connected with his vast business."

3. Henry Hall, ed., *America's Successful Men of Affairs: An Encyclopedia of Contemporaneous Biography* (New York: New York Tribune, 1896), 2:3–4.

4. Ibid., 570.

Chapter 3: Beer Baron Over-the-Rhine

1. See *Cincinnati und sein Deutschthum: Eine Geschichte der Entwickelung Cincinnati's und seines Deutschthums, mit biographischen Skizzen und Illustrationen* (Cincinnati: Queen City Publishing Co., 1901).

2. See William L. Downard, "When Gambrinus was King," *Bulletin of the Cincinnati Historical Society* 29 (1969): 280.

3. See the obituary "Christian Moerlein. 1818–1897," *Vorstands-Bericht des Deutschen Pionier-Vereins von Cincinnati* 29 (1897): 64–67.

4. *Forty-Ninth Annual Report of the Cincinnati Chamber of Commerce and Merchant's Exchange for the Year Ending December 31, 1897* (Cincinnati: The Ohio Valley Company, Printers, 1898), 302–03.

Chapter 4: Cincinnati's Beer Barons

1. For biographical information on Hauck, see Don Henirich Tolzmann, *Over-the-Rhine Tour Guide: Cincinnati's Historic German District and Environs* (Milford, Ohio: Little Miami Pub.Co., 2011), 37–41.

2. Charles F. Goss, *Cincinnati, the Queen City, 1788–1912* (Chicago: S. J. Clarke Pub. Co., 1912), 4:399–401.

3. *History of Cincinnati*, 860–61.

4. Tolzmann, *German Heritage Guide to the Greater Cincinnati Area*, 20, 24, 42, 67, 72–73.

5. Ogle, *Ambitious Brew*, 52.

6. Ibid., 337.

Chapter 5: The Old World

1. Frederic Spotts, *Bayreuth, A History of the Wagner Festival* (New Haven, Conn.: Yale University Press, 1994), 23.

2. Genealogical information on the Moerlein family was provided by Gabriele Zimmermann, e-mail message to author, 25 October 2011.

3. Don Heinrich Tolzmann, *The German-American Experience: A Revised and expanded edition of Theodore Huebener's The Germans in America* (Amherst, N.Y.: Humanity Books, 2000), 152ff.

4. Regarding Ludwig I, see Rudolf Ites and Georg Reichlmayr, *850 Jahre München: Eine kurze Stadtgeschichte*, 2nd rev. ed. (Erfurt: Sutton Verlag, 2008).

5. See Charles F. Goss, *Cincinnati, the Queen City, 1788–1912* (Chicago: S. J. Clarke Pub. Co., 1912), 3:388.

6. For a discussion of the Protestant work ethic, see Max Weber, *The Protestant Work Ethic and the Spirit of Capitalism* (New York: Charles Scribner's Sons, 1930).

7. Tolzmann, *German-American Experience*, 447.

8. Gottfried Duden, *Report on a Journey to the Western States of North America*, ed. James W. Goodrich (Columbia: University of Missouri Press, 1980), 42.

9. A prominent Cincinnati German, Charles Reemelin, wrote, for example, of the importance that Duden's book had in his decision to come to America: "Indeed, I have ever found it to be a reliable guide as to America. It revived and intensified my longings for America." See Charles Reemelin, *Life of Charles Reemelin: in German Carl Gustav Rümelin, from 1814–1892* (Cincinnati: Weier & Daiker, 1892), 22.

10. See: Gustav Koerner, *The German Element in the Northeast: Pennsylvania, New York, New Jersey & New England*, trans., ed. Don Heinrich Tolzmann (Baltimore: Clearfield Company, 2010), 90.

11. For further information on Ziegler and Baum, see Gustav Koerner, *The German Element in the Ohio Valley: Ohio, Kentucky & Indiana*, trans., ed. Don Heinrich Tolzmann (Baltimore: Clearfield Company, 2011), 2–3, 107 and Tolzmann, *German Heritage Guide to the Greater Cincinnati Area*, 47–48.

Chapter 6: The New World

1. Regarding Over-the-Rhine, see Tolzmann, *Over-the-Rhine Tour Guide: Cincinnati's Historic German District and Environs* (Milford, Ohio: Little Miami Publishing Co., 2011).

2. Cited in Don Heinrich Tolzmann, *Cincinnati's German Heritage* (Bowie, Md.: Heritage Books, Inc., 1994), pt. 1, 50.

3. Regarding Wooden Show Hollow, see Charlotte Pieper, *Wooden Shoe Hollow: Charlotte Pieper's Cincinnati German Novel*, 2nd ed., ed. Don Heinrich Tolzmann (Milford, Ohio: Little Miami Pub. Co., 2004).

4. See Tolzmann, *Cincinnati's German Heritage*, pt. 1, 44–47.

5. Henry Howe, *Hamilton County, Ohio: As extracted from Henry Howe's Historical Collections of Ohio*, ed. with new pref. and intro., Barbara Keyser Gargiulo (Milford, Ohio: Little Miami Publishing Co., 2005), 23–24.

6. Ibid., 26.

7. Ibid.

8. Henry Wadsworth Longfellow, *The Poetical Works of Henry Wadsworth Longfellow* (Boston: Houghton, Mifflin and Company, 1884), 222.

Chapter 7: The Soul of the Company

1. See *Cincinnati und sein Deutschthum*, 140.

2. Note that it was common for German-American brewers to send their sons to study at brewing academies and institutes either in Germany or in the United States. For an introduction to the history of German brewing, see Horst Dornbusch, *Prost! The Story of German Beer* (Boulder, Colo.: Siris Books, 1997).

3. Regarding German-Americans and their enthusiasm for the German victory during the Franco-Prussian War that led to the unification of Germany, see Tolzmann, *German-American Experience*, 219–222. Here it is emphasized that "German-Americans praised unification but also the fact that decades of peace followed, as well as the phenomenal progress Germany made in the areas of business, industry, trade, the arts and sciences, social legislation, and international prestige. They basked in the reflected glory, which they appreciated after the hard years of the nativist 1850s

and the trying years of the Civil War. Germany was now a respected nation, and products bearing the stamp 'Made in Germany' translated into quality of the highest order. German-Americans felt they had proved and demonstrated their patriotism and their contributions to America. It had been an uphill struggle, but by 1871 they felt they had earned the right to celebrate that they were now an integral and important part of the nation," 222.

4. Maureen Ogle, *Ambitious Brew*, 125.

5. *Cincinnati und sein Deuthschthum*, 141.

6. Downard, "When Gambrinus was King," 280.

7. For further information, see Zane L. Miller, *Boss Cox's Cincinnati: Urban Politics in the Progressive Era* (Chicago: University of Chicago Press, 1968).

Chapter 8: Showman Par Excellence

1. See George Moerlein, *A Trip Around the World* (Cincinnati: M. & R. Burgheim, 1886), and *Eine Reise um die Welt* (Cincinnati: M. & R. Burgheim, 1886 and 1887).

2. Downard, "When Gambrinus was King," 278, 280.

3. Moerlein, *Trip*, 4.

4. Ibid., 3.

5. Ibid., 4. Note here that Moerlein published travel reports in both the English- and German-language newspapers in Cincinnati. They no doubt served later on as the basis for his travel book, published in English and German language editions.

6. Ibid., 11.

7. Ibid., 4.

8. George Moerlein obviously mixed business with pleasure by meeting with Ferdinand Carl, editor of the *Hopfenzeitung*, the full title of which was *Allgemeine Brauer- und Hopfenzeitung*, a German brewing journal that was published from 1861 to 1943 by the publishing house of Carl in Nuremberg. This was the forerunner of the present-day journal *Brauwelt: Monatsschrift für Brauwissenschaft*, which, since 2007, has been retitled as *Brewing Science: Monatsschrift für Brauwissenschaft*. Moerlein's friendship and visit with Carl demonstrates the close contacts that Moerlein had as a German-American brewer with the brewing industry in Germany.

9. Moerlein here refers to fellow students at the Brewing Academy in Nuremberg, which he attended from 1869 to 1871.

10. This party included his younger brother John, who succeeded George as vice president, and Frank Rattermann, son of the well-known German-American historian in Cincinnati, Heinrich A. Rattermann. For further information on Rattermann, see Mary Edmund Spanheimer, *The German Pioneer Legacy: The Life and Work of Heinrich A. Rattermann*, ed. Don Heinrich Tolzmann. New German-American Studies, vol. 26 (Oxford: Peter Lang Pub. Co., 2004).

11. Moerlein, *Trip*, 175–77.

12. *Atlantic Monthly*, 59 (1887): 285.

13. Frank Y. Grayson, *Pioneers of Night Life on Vine Street* (Cincinnati: 1924), 85.

14. *Cincinnati und sein Deutschthum*, 141.

Chapter 9: The Golden Age

1. See *History of Cincinnati*, 324.

2. *Cincinnati und sein Deutschthum*, 150.

3. Ibid., 139.

4. Regarding Rattermann, see Tenner, 397–402. See also chap. 8, n. 10.

5. Regarding the celebration of German Day and Saengerfest in Cininnati, see Tolzmann, *German Heritage Guide to the Greater Cincinnati Area*, 25, 51–52.

6. Ron Shepherd, e-mail message to author, February 1, 2012.

7. For further information on Jung, see Robert J. Wimberg, *Cincinnati Breweries* (Cincinnati: Ohio Book Store, 1989), 76–78.

8. For an obituary of Jung, see "J. George Jung, Brewer is Dead," *Cincinnati Commercial Tribune*, July 14, 1927.

9. For an obituary of George Moerlein, see "George Moerlein," *Vorstandsbericht des Deutschen Pionier-Vereins* 64 (1931–32): 18.

10. For an obituary of Andrew Moerlein, see "Andrew Moerlein," Vorstandsbericht des Deutschen Pionier-Vereins 47 (1914–15) 72.

11. For a recent history of brewing in the United States, see Ogle, *Ambitious Brew: The Story of American Beer*.

Chapter 10: The Dark Ages

1. Don Heinrich Tolzmann, *Cincinnati's German Heritage*, pt. 1, 105.

2. Don Heinrich Tolzmann, *The Cincinnati Germans After the Great War* (New York: P. Lang, 1987), 185. This book also reprinted in Tolzmann, *Cincinnati's German Heritage*, pt. 3, 185.

3. Ibid., 186–88.

4. See Priscilla Hayes Petty, *Under a Lucky Star: The Story of Frederick A. Hauck* (Cincinnati: Cincinnati Historical Society, 1986).

Chapter 11: The Moerlein Legacy

1. Timothy J. Holian, "An Enduring Cincinnati Legend: The Christian Moerlein Brewing Company," *American Breweriana Journal* (January/February 2001): 26.

2. Auctions of brewing memorabilia have become quite popular in the Greater Cincinnati area. For example, see the following article: "Germania Stein Auction," *German-American News* 15 no. 1 (2009): 2, which describes an auction held at the Germania Society of Cincinnati.

3. For further information about Alger, see Gary Scharnhorst, with Jack Bales, *The Lost Life of Horatio Alger, Jr.* (Bloomington: Indiana University Press, 1985).

4. See J. H. Strasser, *New Ulm, Minnesota: J. H. Strasser's History and Chronology*, trans., ed. Don Heinrich Tolzmann (Milford, Ohio: Little Miami Pub. Co., 2003), 32.

Chapter 12: The Moerlein Renaissance

1. Jeff Waddle, "Greg Hardman: Re-claiming Cincinnati, One Beer at a Time," *Cincinnati Gentlemen*, November/October 2007, 63.

2. For a history of brewing in the region, see the comprehensive history by Timothy Holian cited in chap. 1, n. 9.

3. For further information about Greg Hardman, see Waddle, "Greg Hardman: Re-claiming Cincinnati, One Beer at a Time," *Cincinnati Gentlemen*, November/October 2007, 58–63.

4. Ibid., 60.

5. Quoted in the following article on Oktoberfest: Kurt Iversen, "Living: Home and Leisure," *Cincinnati Enquirer*, October 15, 1972.

6. For further information on the Over-the-Rhine Brewery District, see www.otrbrewerydistrict.org.

7. It should be noted here that the German spelling of the Muhlhauser name included umlauts and was spelled as *Mühlhäuser*. As is often the case, the umlaut was dropped in America. An 1894 history of Cincinnati notes about the Muhlhauser brothers: "The success these gentlemen have met, which is astonishing but, nevertheless, deserving. Strict attention to business, and the placing on the market of beer of the very best quality, soon gained for the firm an enviable reputation. The Windisch and Muhlhauser boys are well known over the entire country and State. Being young men, always ready to help a friend in distress, it did not take long to build up for them a lucrative trade. Today the brewery is one of the largest in the country, manufacturing no less than five brands of beer: The Lager, the Pilsener, the Standard, the Lion Brew and the Lion Export. The latter being bottled beer only. The brewery, the product of which is shipped into ten different States, is situated on Liberty, Wade and Fifteenth streets, having a frontage of 1,100 feet on both sides of the canal. In the first year 20,000 barrels were brewed, in 1868, 30,000 barrels, in 1880, 100,000 barrels, and in 1892, 175,000 barrels. Gottlieb Muhlhauser is president of the company; Henry Muhlhauser, vice-president; Henry Muhlhauser, Jr., treasurer; Charles F. Windisch, secretary; William A. Windisch, assistant secretary, and Edward Muhlhauser, brewmaster." See *History of Cincinnati and Hamilton County, Ohio*, 324.

8. For a survey of Cincinnati's brewing history, see Lisa Bernard-Kuhn, "Brewers built jobs, fortunes, legacy on empires of suds," *Cincinnati Enquirer*, February 19, 2012.

Chapter 13: Moerlein Heritage Tour

1. Regarding brewery architecture, see Susan K. Appel, "Buildings and Beer: Brewery Architecture in Cincinnati," *Queen City Heritage* (Summer 1986): 3–21.

2. Regarding Spring Grove, see Phillip J.Nuxhall, *Beauty in the Grove: Spring Grove Cemetery and Arboretum* (Wilmington,Ohio: Orange Frazier Press, 2010). And for a biography of Adolph Strauch, the well-known nineteenth-century superintendent of Spring Grove who exerted a decisive impact on its layout and design, see H. A. Rattermann, *Spring Grove and its Creator: H.A. Rattermann's Biography of Adolph Strauch*, ed. Don Heinrich Tolzmann (Cincinnati: Ohio Book Store, 1988).

Appendix A: Fellow Beer Barons

1. Jung's brewery closed down with the onset of Prohibition.

2. Regarding the Herancourt Brewing Company, see Robert J. Wimberg, *Cincinnati Breweries*, 60–64. An 1894 history of Cincinnati provides the following information regarding this brewery: "Cincinnati's Oldest Brewery—The Herancourt Brewing Company is the oldest brewery in Cincinnati, having been established in 1840. The plant is located on Harrison Avenue, near Brighton Station, having a frontage of 640 feet on Harrison Avenue, and an average depth of 350 feet, comprising about six acres in all, and covering the original site. The business was originally carried on under the firm name of The G. M. Herancourt Brewery, but assumed its present title in 1881 on the incorporation of the company with a capital of $500,000. The output for the first year was 600 barrels; last year it exceeded 35,000. The executives at present are R. Lutterby, president and treasurer; Casimer Work, vice-president; Robert H. Herancourt, secretary; Louis A. Herancourt, superintendent, the remaining directors being B. Herancourt, F. Egner, M. Egner, John Hauck and M. Schwartz." See *History of Cincinnati*, 329–30.

3. Regarding the Koehler Brewery and its relationship with other breweries, the 1894 history of Cincinnati notes that "About nine years ago Louis Hudepohl and George Kotte formed a partnership to engage in the brewery business, and established a plant on the site years ago occupied by the Koehler Brewery, Buckeye Street, now called Clifton Avenue. When they first went into business the building was a comparatively small one, but the sale of their beer increased so rapidly that in a few years they were compelled to erect a much larger one, and to-day it is the handsomest building in that vicinity. It is a pressed brick building, and has frontage of 240 feet and a depth of 120 feet. The capacity of the brewery is 100,000 barrels per year. In 1886 the output was 25,000 barrels; in 1890, 40,000 barrels, and during the last three years the sales have been increased to such an extent that to-day it, ranks as one of the largest breweries in the State." See ibid, 329. See also Wimberg, *Cincinnati Breweries*, 83.

4. The Windisch-Mühlhäuser brewery was another casualty of Prohibition.

5. The Kauffman Brewery also closed as a result of Prohibition.

6. By going through Robert J. Wimberg's directory of area breweries the author identified the places of origin of area brewers. See Wimberg, *Cincinnati Breweries*.

Appendix B: Lager Beer History

1. Hermann Schlüter (1876–1916) served as editor of the *New Yorker Volkszeitung*.

2. Ogle, *Ambitious Brew*, 12.

3. Holian, *Over the Barrel*, 1:39.

Appendix C: Major Breweries in Greater Cincinnati

1. See *History of Cincinnati and Hamilton County, Ohio* (Cincinnati: S. B. Nelson & Co., Publishers; S. B. Nelson, J. M. Runk, 1894).

2. See *They Built a City: 150 Years of Industrial Cincinnati*, comp. and written by the Cincinnati Federal Writers' Project of the Works Progress Administration in Ohio (Cincinnati: The Cincinnati Post, 1938), 135–36.

Sources

SOURCES FOR THIS BIOGRAPHY of Christian Moerlein can be found in the endnotes to the various chapters throughout this work, but several are worthy of taking note of here. German-language histories of the Cincinnati Germans were especially important as sources of biographical information on the Moerlein family. And the most useful were Armin Tenner, *Cincinnati Sonst und Jetzt: Eine Geschichte Cincinnati's und seiner verdienstvollen Bürger deutscher Zunge, mit biographischen Skizzen und Portrait Illustrationen* (Cincinnati: Druck von Mecklenborg & Rosenthal, 1878); Max Burgheim, *Cincinnati in Wort und Bild* (Cincinnati: M. & R. Burgheim, 1888); and *Cincinnati und sein Deutschthum: Eine Geschichte der Entwickelung Cincinnati's und seines Deutschthums, mit biographischen Skizzen und Illustrationen* (Cincinnati: Queen City Publishing Co., 1901). All of these were written by contemporaries of Moerlein who more than likely knew him personally. Additionally, the annual reports of the German Pioneer Society of Cincinnati, the *Vorstandsberichte des Deutschen Pioniervereins von Cincinnati*, were quite informative for the biographical information they contained.

By way of comparison with German-American sources two English-language sources were quite useful in showing how Moerlein was portrayed in a regional, as well as national biographical work: The *History of Cincinnati and Hamilton County, Ohio* (Cincinnati: S. B. Nelson & Co., Publishers; S. B. Nelson, J. M. Runk, 1894) and: Henry Hall, ed., *America's Successful Men of Affairs: An Encyclopedia of Contemporaneous Biography* (New York: New

York Tribune, 1896).

Since members of the Moerlein family belonged to the German-American societies of the area, the following two directories were helpful for the information they provide on their histories: August Gorbach, *Deutscher Vereins-Wegweiser von Cincinnati* (Cincinnati: S. Rosenthal & Co., 1915) and also his *Das Hilfswerk und Cincinnatis deutsche Vereine* (Cincinnati: S. Rosenthal, 1917).

Works by the author are cited in the endnotes, but the following were those that were most useful for this biography: *Over-the-Rhine Tour Guide: Cincinnati's Historic German District and Environs* (Milford, Ohio: Little Miami Pub. Co., 2011); *German Cincinnati* (Charleston, S.C.: Arcadia Publishing, 2005); *German Cincinnati Revisited* (Charleston, S.C.: Arcadia Publishing, 2011); *Cincinnati's German Heritage* (Bowie, Md.: Heritage Books, Inc., 1994); and *German-Americana: Selected Essays* (Milford, Ohio: Little Miami Pub. Co., 2009).

Finally, two works were useful for understanding the place of the Moerlein Brewing Company within the brewing industry locally and nationally: Timothy J. Holian's *Over the Barrel: The Brewing History and Beer Culture of Cincinnati, 1800 to the Present* (St. Joseph, Mo.: Sudhaus Press, 2000–2001) covers the Cincinnati scene up to the recent past, while Maureen Ogle's *Ambitious Brew: The Story of American Beer* (Orlando, Fla.: Harcourt Inc., 2006) does likewise on a national scale.

Acknowledgments

SOMETIME AFTER THE PUBLICATION OF MY BOOK *John A. Roebling and His Suspension Bridge on the Ohio River* (Milford, Ohio: Little Miami Publishing Co., 2007), my good friend Greg Hardman, president and CEO of the Christian Moerlein Brewing Company, contacted me while he was in Germany, inquiring if I might be interested in doing a biography of Christian Moerlein. After he got back to Cincinnati, we met at Arnold's Bar and Grill on Eighth Street to discuss the project. We then took a tour of several sites in the Over-the-Rhine district, including the old Moerlein Brewery. I readily agreed that Moerlein was deserving of a biography. Although I had other works in progress at the time, I indicated that I would eventually like to work on such a project. I would like to thank him for bringing this fascinating topic to my attention and also for discussing it with me as work on this biography proceeded on to completion. Also, I would like to thank him for writing the foreword to this volume and also for contributing the timeline of the Christian Moerlein Brewing Company for this work.

Thanks also to Anne Shepherd, reference librarian at the Cincinnati Historical Society for her assistance at the historical society. Also many thanks to her husband, Ron, whose great-grandfather's brother, J. George Jung, was a nephew of Christian Moerlein and served as the last president of the Christian Moerlein Brewing Company. Both introduced me to Carl Hilker, whose mother, Ella, was married to Jacob Moerlein, a grandson of Christian Moerlein. After Jacob's death, Ella remarried and Carl was raised with his half brother George Moerlein at the Moerlein farm in Butler County. Meeting together with the Shepherds and Carl Hilker provided me with information and recollections about the Moerlein family that were most helpful.

I also spoke with two direct descendants, Tim and Andy Moerlein—the former lives in Alaska, and the latter in New Hampshire. Thanks to them for the information they provided, as well as to Steve Moerlein for the information he provided about the family. I would especially like to express gratitude to Gabriele Mörlein Zimmermann of Mistelgau, Germany, who provided me with records from the archives of the Evangelical-Lutheran Church of Bavaria relating to the early history of the Moerlein family.

Thanks also to Fred Knodle for the picture of Moerlein Brewery workers toasting Christian Moerlein on the occasion of his death; Kevin Grace, University of Cincinnati, for the picture of the Moerlein Brewery; and Daniel Nützel, Indiana University-Purdue University at Indianapolis, for pictures of the village of Truppach in Upper Franconia. I would also like to thank Jerry Glenn, editor of the German Heritage Museum Lecture Series, for his reading of the manuscript and his many helpful recommendations for its improvement.

Finally, I would like to thank the Little Miami Publishing Company for its great support in bringing out this and other works of mine dealing with the German heritage. For further information about them, see its website at www.littlemiamibooks.com.

Don Heinrich Tolzmann
Cincinnati, Ohio
Spring 2012

Index

About the Author

DR. DON HEINRICH TOLZMANN is the author and editor of numerous books on German-American history and culture. He has received many awards, including the Cross of Merit from the Federal Republic of Germany, the Distinguished German-American of the Year Award, the Ohioana Book Award, and the SGAS Outstanding Achievement Award from the Society for German-American Studies. He has led the movement to create an awareness of America's German heritage and promoted German-American Studies and the strengthening of relations between Germany and the United States. Until retirement, he served as curator of the German-Americana Collection and director of the German-American Studies Program at the University of Cincinnati.

As president of the Society for German-American Studies he called for the celebration of the German-American Tricentennial in

1983, marking the establishment of the first German settlement in America at Germantown, Pennsylvania, and in 1987 led the national campaign to establish October 6 as national German-American Day, earning him the title of "Father of German-American Day." In 1989, he organized the first German-American Heritage Month in Cincinnati, Ohio, and since that time has actively promoted the national celebration during the month of October. He also initiated plans for the celebration of the 400th anniversary of the arrival of the first Germans in America at Jamestown, Virginia, in 2008. Dr. Randall Donaldson (Loyola University) has called him "the dean of German-American Studies, and Dr. Jerry Glenn (University of Cincinnati) notes that he "has little competition for the title 'Mr. German-Americana.'"

He edits a monographic book series *New German-American Studies/Neue deutsch-amerikanische Studien*, published by the Peter Lang Publishing Company and serves on the editorial board of the *Yearbook of German-American Studies*, as well as many other publications, and serves as book review editor of *German Life*.

As an active, dedicated, and informed member and officer of many regional and national German-American organizations, he has frequently been called upon to represent German-American interests in Washington, D.C. He has served on the boards of many international, national, and regional organizations and institutions, including the German Emigration Center/Deutsches Auswandererhaus in Bremerhaven, Germany, and the Friends of the German Historical Institute in Washington, D.C.

He has served as president of several organizations, including the Society for German-American Studies and currently is president of the German-American Citizens League of Greater Cincinnati and curator of its German Heritage Museum in Cincinnati. He also serves on the boards of the Covington-Cincinnati Suspension Bridge Committee, the Steuben Society of America, the German-American Hall of Fame, and the Beer Barons Hall of Fame.

Printed by Publishers' Graphics LLC USA